BREAD LOAF

ANTHOLOGY

PREFACE BY ROBERT FROST

MIDDLEBURY COLLEGE PRESS - MIDDLEBURY VERMONT
1939

In Memory of
JOSEPH BATTELL

ACKNOWLEDGMENTS

For permission to reprint certain poems in this book to which credit lines are attached the Middlebury College Press is indebted to editors of the following: *American Prefaces; Christian Register; Christian Science Monitor; Good Will Record;* Middlebury *News Letter; New Yorker;* New York Herald *Tribune;* New York Post; New York Times; *Poetry; Razón de Amor; Saturday Review of Literature; Scholastic; Spirit; Upward; Voices; Zion's Herald.*

INTRODUCTION

The Mountain had first claim to the name Bread Loaf. The farm, the Inn, the summer village, the School, the Little Theatre, a library, the Writers' Conference,—and now a book—all borrowed from the mountain. Most of them have borrowed more than a name.

In 1850 "Bread Loaf" was a desolate upland farm—an outpost in the mountain wilderness of central Vermont. To the north rose Bread Loaf Mountain shaped against the horizon not unlike the double brown loaves still being baked in a few Vermont chimney ovens. The only signs of encroaching civilization were the lumber wagons which thundered over the narrow mountain road carrying logs to the Ripton and Middlebury mills, and the Boston stage coach which still ran in competition with the new railroad on the valley route. The only signs of neighbors were the lights which flickered across the valley at night from the Widow's Clearing to the south and from still higher clearings across Brandy Brook to the north. The Bread Loaf farmhouse was un-distinguished from the half dozen other pioneer houses on the upper grades of the mountain pass.

Twenty years later Bread Loaf had become a famous mountain resort in the true provincial-Victorian tradition. Its select, but oddly demo-cratic clientele from Boston, New York, Washington, and from lesser towns and cities of New England had begun to agree that the Inn ad-vertisements, if anything, were an understatement of what Bread Loaf Inn actually offered. Those advertisements, a good half column in length, were obviously written by no press agent with a flair for journalese. They were honest, calculated essays:

> Having succeeded in securing competent help for every department of the Hotel, we no longer hesitate to recommend the Bread Loaf Inn to all who seek a place for recreation, amusement, health or enjoyment. Mr. Caleb Ticknor, now of Great Barrington, Mass., but formerly of the Addison House and so well known as one of the most successful and accomplished landlords of our state, said lately of a dinner at the Bread Loaf Inn that it was the best that he had ever sat down to at a country hotel.

Although so high a compliment from such an authority was unexpected to us, we believe that the Bread Loaf Inn will maintain its reputation, and in its culinary department, henceforth rank with Hyde's Hotel as one of the best in the country.

The situation of the Bread Loaf Inn is peculiarly adapted to enjoyment. One finds himself removed here to a higher atmosphere of entirely different life from that which he has been accustomed to. The novelty charms, the freshness fascinates, the decided character pleases, the walks delight, the mountains impress, and their air cool, clear, bracing, invigorates.

Near to the Bread Loaf Inn, is the Bread Loaf Mountain, constantly urging the adventurous spirit to explore its wilds, or the man of action to conquer its distance. After this might be mentioned the drive from Ripton along the fern-lined, brook-crossed roads, and through the wilderness to the exquisite valley in which Lincoln lies; and the scarcely marked but more easily traveled route over the Hancock mountain to the White river.

Within an afternoon's walk of the Inn is Burnt Hill, one of the finest points of view in the State and Hancock pond upon the top of the mountain. Within an hour's stroll is Bisby Hill whence Lake Champlain is visible, the retired locality of Goshen river; the lover's walk to the old mill. Trout streams everywhere.

A good livery is joined to the hotel with saddle horses for ladies and gentlemen. Guests will find, too, at the hotel a superior spyglass and field glass; different games of cards, chess, etc., croquet, footballs, quoits, fishing tackle, and facilities for target shooting with rifle or revolver. In addition to these, there are daily, semi-weekly, weekly, and monthly periodicals in a library, piano, with several volumes of carefully chosen songs, and a very choice collection of photographic slides.

Dinners hereafter at the Bread Loaf Inn will be $1. Otherwise our terms will remain as hitherto advertised, $10 per week, $2 per day, although next year we shall intend to raise them somewhat as inadequate to the amount of entertainment offered.

The hospitality was not limited to the summer months. As a center for winter sports in the European tradition, Bread Loaf was to wait for more than half a century, but thanks to an ingenious snow roller which kept the roads packed and icy, the Inn was a favorite destination for sleigh parties of Middlebury town and gown revelers. The winter advertisements ran:

> Dinner 75 cts.; Oyster Suppers, $1; board per day, $2; feed for horse, 50c. We have recently added to our accommodations a Ball Room, 45 x 24, which enables us to accommodate large evening parties for dancing, and other country amusements. The Bread Loaf Inn has so large a regular summer business now, that we are obliged at that season to place our day charges high. During the winter we make them as low as we can afford for the benefit of sleighing parties and local custom.

The lord of this grand country hotel of the late 1800's was Joseph Battell who on the abundant largess supplied by a wealthy relative could afford to play country squire. Joseph had gone to the desolate mountain farmhouse for a weekend, had stayed on indefinitely, bought the house, the farm, the surrounding forests; and started inviting his friends, their friends and friends of friends to join him as "guests." The oddest thing about the popular Inn was the management: it was run as an overgrown private home. Joseph Battell knew no pecuniary standards of hospitality. He himself met the guests at Middlebury, twelve miles distant, drove them himself in the two-seated coach to Bread Loaf, handled their bags, escorted them to their rooms, lit their kerosene lamps, personally planned and supervised sumptuous meals and entertained them with reminiscence and gruff wit around one of the numerous Inn hearths. There were no bell hops, no tips, frequently no bills. If the Manager-owner didn't go into the red to the extent of several hundred or even several thousand dollars during the summer it was considered an unsuccessful season.

But Battell's interests were not limited to hotel management. Education, architecture, horsebreeding, higher mathematics and physics, editing and publishing, authorship, photography, road and bridge construction, cartography, politics, European travel, and forest conservation all shared places with this man who was so many men. For over thirty years he edited and published the Middlebury *Register*, waging incessant war on the invasion of Vermont by a machine age. He discovered the original Morgan horse, and bought a farm near Middlebury where its offspring could be propagated, first under his own direction and later by the United States Government. He published the first *American Stallion Register*, and did another scholarly volume on the Morgan horse. His romanticised books on mathematics, physics, and philosophy were less scholarly, but no less intense. For eight terms he served in the Vermont Legislature and for thirty-four years as trustee of Middlebury College, to which he donated a new campus for the Women's College as well as the first two dormitories for women.

But his most consuming interest was in Vermont forest conservation in an age when conservation was a new word in New England and when a pioneer in that field was considered economically if not socially irregular. In Europe as early as the 1860's, Battell had made his first observations on forest preservation but the application to the Green Mountains was not driven home until one morning from the Bread Loaf porch he saw a woodchopper slashing into a nearby timber lot. The uncomfortable thought dawned on him; one day these thousands of acres seen from his Inn might be scarred by great ugly patches of cut land. Erosion would follow, dried streams, forest fires. His friends were paying $10,000 for paintings to hang on their walls. Why not buy the subject instead of the reproduction and preserve it for all time? He could buy a whole mountain for less than $10,000. With typical guarded impetuosity he advanced to the wood lot with his wallet and bought the land on the spot. Then with his dream of preserving the wealth of Bread Loaf scenery for posterity he began purchasing wild lands at fifty, twenty-five, even ten cents an acre. Rates slowly rose with the demand. Hundreds of acres he bought at $1.25—any plot within view of the Inn. Most of Monastery Mountain, Worth Peak, Boyce Mountain, Bread Loaf, Roosevelt, Grant, Lincoln Mountain, and Camel's Hump he secured in the course of a few years until he owned more territory than any other individual in Vermont.

When the connoisseur of mountains died in 1915 his holdings amounted to some 40,000 acres. Most of them were willed to Middlebury College, his alma mater, along with Bread Loaf Inn, his publishing company and newspaper, and a whole business block in Middlebury.

Time has seen the value of the vast estate multiply, though the donor could never have anticipated the innumerable benefits which would accrue from it. Shortly after his death Bread Loaf became the home of the English School which was being crowded off the campus by the new summer language schools of German, Spanish and French. And in 1923 the Writers' Conference became a new Bread Loaf institution. Recently part of the mountain area was sold to the United States Government, which could better afford to preserve the reservation, and the income went into an immense dormitory, appropriately named Forest Hall. Even the Bread Loaf winter sports center with its cabin and adjacent runs can be attributed to him. There is hardly a department of Middlebury College that has not been assisted directly or indirectly by the Battell benefactions.

The Bread Loaf School of English and the Bread Loaf Writers' Conference are perhaps the most significant manifestations of the Battell legacy. Both were started as institutions unique in the educational field. The curriculum for the School over a period of years touches the whole range of English and American literature as well as the relation of these to philosophy and the other arts, while the annual two weeks Writers' Conference emphasizes creative writing and manuscript criticism. Many books and hundreds of poems, articles, and stories have been published as a by-product of the training and criticism offered at the English School and the Conference. As Mr. Hervey Allen has noted, Bread Loaf has become "a common meeting ground for the experiencing and tasting of the living literature of the past and the live literature of the present."

Today that desolate little mountain farmstead which Battell purchased in the '60's has expanded into a small summer village, a literary school and colony complete with its Post Office, Little Theatre, Library, Book Store, central campus and a long row of houses. And true to the Battell wishes, the thousands of acres of mountain and forest land lie unbroken, exactly as they were three quarters of a century ago.

All too frequently the origin of individual legacies is forgotten. They are caught up among the great number of bequests—social, ideological, pecuniary—which together give individuality to an institution. This book is published on the hundredth birthday of Joseph Battell as an acknowledgement of the inventive and pioneer spirit of the greatest benefactor of Middlebury College and Bread Loaf. His generosity, the strong character, his expression of the Vermont ideal will long survive him.

Some of these ideals are voiced in the poems. Beyond that they represent some of the fruit of Battell's benefactions, work contributed by Bread Loaf English students and staff, members of the Writers' Conference, and alumni and faculty of Middlebury College.

The generosity with which authors contributed is in itself an expression of their regard for Joseph Battell and Bread Loaf. The publication of the volume is philanthropic throughout. Mr. Ben Lane of the Lane Press has assumed the entire cost of printing and illustrating the book. Robert Frost, a member of the lecturing staff at Bread Loaf since 1921, has contributed the preface. And the judges and committee in charge have given generously of their time and energy. These include, beside Mr. Frost, Harry G. Owen, Donald Davidson, and Theodore Morrison.

W. STORRS LEE, *Editor*

CONTENTS

LIST OF ILLUSTRATIONS

Illustrations by Edward Sanborn

THE DOCTRINE OF EXCURSIONS
A PREFACE

You who are as much concerned as I for the future of Bread Loaf will agree with me that once in so often it should be redefined if it is to be kept from degenerating into a mere summer resort for routine education in English, or worse still for the encouragement of vain ambition in literature. We go there not for correction or improvement. No writer has ever been corrected into importance. Nor do we go to find a publisher or get help in finding a publisher. Bringing manuscript to Bread Loaf is in itself publication.

A writer can live by writing to himself alone for days and years. Sooner or later to go on he must be read. It may well be that in appealing to the public he has but added to his own responsibility; for now besides judging himself he must judge his judges. For long the public received him not. Then the public received him. When were the public right? Why, when the final authority is his, should he be bothered with any other? The answer is an article in the doctrine of excursions. All we know is that the crowning mercy for an author is publication in some form or other.

Undeniably the best form is a book with a reputable house at the expense of the house. The next best is a book with a reputable house at the expense of the author. Those two constitute publication in the first and second degrees. But there are several humbler degrees, among them the Bread Loaf Conference. It must not be forgotten that much good poetry has never risen above the second degree and some has undoubtedly come out in newspapers that pay nothing for contributions. Publication in book form like this anthology of ours was not contemplated in the original scheme of Bread Loaf and is not of the essence of the institution. It has simply been added unto us as a reward for modesty.

Bread Loaf is to be regarded then as a place in Vermont where a writer can try his effect on readers. There, as out in the world, he must brave the rigors of specific criticism. He will get enough and perhaps more than enough of good set praise and blame. He will help wear out the words "like" and "dislike." He will hear too many things compared to the disadvantage of all of them. A handkerchief is worse than a knife because it can be cut by a knife; a knife is worse than a stone because it can be blunted by a stone; a stone is worse than a handkerchief because it can be covered by a handkerchief; and we have been round the silly circle. All this is as it has to be where the end is a referee's decision. There is nothing so satisfactory in literature as the knock-out in prize fighting.

But more than out in the world a writer has a chance at Bread Loaf of getting beyond this cavil and getting his proof of something better than approval in signs—looks, tones, manners. Many words are often but one small sign. There is the possibility of his winning through to the affections of the affectionate.

Beyond the self-esteem and the critical opinion of others, the scientist has a third proof I have envied for the artist. From the perturbation of a planet in its orbit he predicts exactly where in the sky and at what time of night another planet will be discovered. All telescopes point that way and there the new planet is. The scientist is justified of his figures. He knows he is good. He has fitted into the nature of the universe. A typical play of the eighties had in it a scene from the digging of the Hoosac Tunnel. The engineer had triangulated over the mountains and driven in shafts from opposite sides to meet each other under the middle of the mountain. It was the eleventh hour of the enterprise. There stood the engineer among the workmen in one shaft waiting to hear from the workmen in the other. A gleam of pickaxe broke through; a human face appeared in the face of the rock. The engineer was justified of his figures. He knew he was an engineer. He had fitted into the nature of the universe.

I should like to believe the poet gets an equivalent assurance in the affections of the affectionate. He has fitted into the nature of mankind. He is justified of his numbers. He has acquired friends who will even cheat for him a little and refuse to see his faults if they are not so glaring as to show through eyelids. And friends are everything. For why have we wings if not to seek friends at an elevation?

ROBERT FROST

ANNIE McCONKUS

A Legend of the Aroostook War

Amy Belle Adams

Annie McConkus flirted the rag in the pan
And hung it to dry over the wooden sink
That Pat had made her so long ago—"A man
If ever there was one!" she whispered, and smiled to think
Of their lusty youth when he felled the towering trees
And laid them up for the walls and chinked the cracks
With moss. How red was his hair in the sun and breeze!
Now he was dead and gone, and hers was the axe.
But the clearing shrank each year, for she was old
And tired of keeping a roadhouse here in the cold;
Tired of border war that had just begun
Since Maine and New Brunswick both were cutting the spruce
And calling each other thief. "Fighting is fun
For the young and the Irish," she said, "but what's the use?"
Little she thought that before the end of night
She'd prove that the Irish are never too old to fight.
At the squeak of runners she ran to open the door.
Horses and sleds were filling the yard, and men
Swarmed through the dusk to stamp their feet on her floor.
Ten and twenty and thirty: she counted again.
"We'll want some supper," the Province leader said.
"MacKenzie and Harris, bring in the guns and packs."
"This time tomorrow we'll be at the lake or dead,"
Growled one. "If the snow doesn't fill the tracks
Too deep for sledding," rejoined a quiet lad
Who blew on the frosted pane to see the flakes.
Their voices mingled: "We'll teach the Yanks." . . . "I'm glad
To smell some beans a-cooking." . . . "My shoulder aches."

She set the table and fed them and listened hard
To the scraps of talk that strengthened her early fear;
By the time they were bedded aloft and the door was barred
The thing that she had to do was crystal-clear.
Over her widow's cap she fastened a shawl,
Another about her shoulders. She thought of her cow
But feared lest she waken the men with her friendly bawl.
" 'Tis a shame for her to go hungry with hay in the mow, . . .
But praise to the saints for the dark of night!"
She thought, as she inched her way through the door
And closed it softly. She dared not carry a light.
If she found where the tote-road forked, she would ask no more.
The snowflakes against her face were soft and cold.
She thought of the sixteen miles that lay before
And prayed for the strength of the young and the will of the old.
What could the Maine men do when her message was told?
She trusted to them for that. Her job was to take
One step through the snow and another. The tops of the trees
Showed her the turn-off. She knew she must make
Better time than this. She could feel no breeze.
The snow had ceased and the clouds were beginning to break.
No need to ponder the cause of the present raid:
When Provincials had cut the spruce by the lake she sought,
The State-of-Mainers who owned the land had made
A canal to drain the lake away, so caught
The "timber thieves" with their lumber high and dry.
" 'Twas a clever trick," she thought, with a tired sigh.
The wall of trees on her right was replaced by the gray
Of a frozen wind-swept lake. The feathery snow
Blinded, half-choked her, swirling. She knew the way
And plodded with desperate haste. Surely the men
At the camp would know of help they could get somewhere.

Her mind grew cloudy; she staggered and dozed again,
But spurred herself with the thought she was nearly there.
The Cut Lake garrison woke to the steady thump
Of mittened fists against the boards of the door,
And a shrill voice crying, "War!" With a bump
Two dozen feet together struck the floor.
At four in the morning Annie had eaten and slept.
The messenger sent to Loveland's had only now
Returned with reinforcements. Nothing kept
Her, she thought, from sauntering home to feed the cow.
In an hour or so she came to the lake again.
Head bowed against the wind, she plowed along
Straight into the midst of the marching Province men;
In desperation she fought to escape the throng.
But an axe came crashing down on the old brown shawl.
Stars shot fire and faded. She never would know
Of the others' shamed dismay when they saw her fall
Upon her face in the cold and yielding snow.
As bitter dawn was breaking, the skirmish began;
Their surprise a failure, their forces now too few,
The Province raiders dropped their arms and ran,
While the yelling Yankees waved their guns to pursue.
Over the miles where Annie had staggered, they flew
Like boys out of school; but a grim and sudden hush
Settled upon them as one by one they knew
The lifeless heap that lay in the alder brush.
At the foot of the frozen lake they dug a grave.
And buried the woman they came too late to save.
Annie McConkus Lake the old maps say:
To Amaconcus it changed—Umcolcus today.
Long was her story told, forgotten, and then
Revived and shaped from the shattered fragments again.

Peace to her ashes and peace to the neighboring North;
With blame for none we set her story forth—
Only to lend her fame to the printed page,
To write her name on the maps of a newer age.
For we who have heard her story told at night
When the frost is deep on the pane and the fire is bright,
Hearing the roar of wind, ... shiver and start,
Dreaming of lonely miles and an Irish heart.

"Annie McConkus" was chosen for the award of $100, among the long poems submitted for *The Bread Loaf Anthology*.

THE EARTH MOVES

Amy Belle Adams

In spring you've leaned upon the weathered rail
Of some old bridge where foaming water sped,
And watched until you saw the current rest
While bridge and you went floating on instead.
Though taking the world on such a heavenly sail
Is something strange I've never heard nor read,
I've seen it move, as Galileo said.

Deep evening silhouetted tops of trees
Against the afterglow that lit the sky;
Upon the narrow porch as on a deck,
I watched the wreaths of ragged fog-cloud fly,
Swiftly as waves before a lusty breeze
Careening past the post I marked them by.
Then for a moment only, porch and I,

The whole dark yard and trees began to roam:
Earth slipped her moorings or the cable parted.
Setting her course by the lighted evening star,
Into the wind-swept, watery sky she darted.
And now when I am stranded here at home,
This much is solace: that at least I started
Upon a course that's never yet been charted.

AFTERGLOW

Hervey Allen

Come dance with me, ye everlasting hills,
Not less firm fixed within our father's hand
My soul doth lie within my body sweet—
Sweet as a lake held in the hollow land.

And though, ye hills, ye move in ampler time
Than my two feet can ever find the way,
My soul can foot it with you rhyme for rhyme,
For it shall be when you have danced away.

THE PRICE OF LIBERTY

Florence Becker

I. To Any Living Writer

The elasticity of the horizon is remarkable;
Sometimes the farthest nebula of Hercules will not overtax it
Or it may contract and snap around your forehead—
A tight black band.
There are still people who can clamp it like the iron maiden
To match the one they wear.

Then hasten
Never let it catch.
They have worn it like that from infancy
But you would not survive.

Some have thought to save themselves on the narrow island between
    two oceans
In the labyrinth where the doors bang and empty masks swing in the wind
Where dead voices cry old songs and nothing has a name.
But the water washes in from both oceans
And this is the time of few words and clear—
"On the one hand—on the other hand"—has gone to roost with the
    archaeopteryx.

Between you and the inkwell is only that sheet of white paper
Waiting, waiting.
On the shelves behind you are massed your armies;
Behind your forehead the general is asleep.

Wake up!
The paper is the plain of Marathon,
It is you who must stem the ten thousand.
All we have wrested from darkness since the standing erect of
    pithecanthropos
Is caught in that tightening ring of iron.

Muster your little force—no matter!
Thermopylae was lost through treachery, not lack of reinforcements.

The white paper plain will swell and widen,
Ink merges imperceptibly into blood
And the little pen-wavers are lost in the gathering armies
Marching indomitably on the barbarian lictors.

The days of our impotence are over
And we are chosen to triumph or to die;
Meanwhile there are simples and incantations against contraction of the
  horizon:
REMEMBER — BELIEVE — HOPE — ACT SWIFTLY.

First Intermezzo

Tolerance

The enemy
They have their heroes too
Their honest men
But best of all, their seers
Who impeccably perceive
The tips of their own noses
And the backs of their own ears.

Snout of pig and tooth of wolf
Strut of cock and swoop of vulture
That is human nature.

A man must believe what he sees in the mirror.

II. Remember

The caryatides of the Erechtheion
Uphold the blue bowl of the sky.
The flowers in the footprints of Persephone

Cushioned Sappho's lilting feet—
Those brown feet pulsing on the grass,
Those brown small fingers on the lyre—
The dawn-bird singing.
(Even the dawn, even the very dawn-bird
Knew bipedal beasts of burden with no music in their feet—
The free resting on the unfree.)
They who pluck the nettles from the grass
They shall not dance—not yet.

Or let it be Georgian London—
Lord Elgin raped the Parthenon—
(Say rather that immaculate conception brought forth Endymion.)
Who knows what apothecary's apprentice has seen Persephone
Or what son of a baronet has heard the west wind calling?
From the songs of Sappho to the Grecian Urn is all one dance—
(Counting in light-years and thought-waves)
But from the slaves of Lesbos to the children spinning cotton out of
          their bodies in Manchester
Stretches a different kind of time.

Yonder on the peak of the past century
The last bright figures flash across the clouds;
The chain of dancers passes from the pediment of the Parthenon
Leaping over the valley of Victoria—
The Irish girl from San Francisco touches the Grecian Urn
And bare feet feel the grass again.
This time it is not enough:
She has heard the broken boots of the burden bearers
Without whose daughters there shall be no dance.
(From Spartacus on the slopes of Vesuvius
To Spartacus Unter der Linden is barely a bird call away.)

Isadora brushes the future with her scarf
Evoking a television of the gait and stature implicit in our heritage;

The flowers of Persephone will uphold our feet
When we become the burden-sharers.

Second Intermezzo

By the Beard of the Prophet

Man is a divinity second to none
He pierces the stratosphere
Unveils pockets of darkness around the corner from the universe
And once he was even Beethoven.
But he has a point of weakness—
On that point how many angels have split their slippers!
He has an engine that must be stoked;
Oxygen he requires
And bricks of sun-stuff for his combustion.

On this point all wars are constructed
And he who can master this pointed needle
Will mend the shoes of all the dancing angels.
There will be no mending now;
Pull the dust-cover over the harp
And hide it under the staircase—
The wind of darkness is blowing.

Such a wind as never was before
The wind that blew the Goths down over the Apennines into Rome
Is nothing to it;
The wind that blew Jenghis Khan over the plains of Asia to the Silesian
      forest
That was not so black.

A little twister got loose in Sarajevo
Blew up into a hurricane
Subsided.
Here it comes again—somebody ripped a parachute in Ethiopia

And all the little winds came spilling out
Spinning up faster and faster over Barcelona
Whipping up wilder and wilder waltzes over Shanghai
And now it's LOOSE!

We may firmly expect our hair to blow off with our hats
(With or without our heads—we shall see.)
The house will undoubtedly go spinning off toward Andromeda
(Including the staircase)
But if any of us are here afterwards
We shall need the harp.

The foetuses leap from the womb saluting the dictator,
The tea-leaves prophesy the end of the world,
The crocuses in the window-box expect bone fertilizer.
Leave the gas-cocks on and let the bath-tub run over—
As well now as next week—

And yet—
On Seventh Avenue there is a commotion
The people are pouring out of the subway
The power is shut off
The power is shut off
THE POWER IS SHUT OFF!

The power—where is it now?
But where has it always been?
The power is in our hands.

III. Believe

A man alone is not a monument
He can not stand.
His poise must be the poise of motion—
The little triangle behind his toes will hold him
But not too long
And not alone.

He cracked a thousand words to find one thought;
Now can he hold it?
If he can remember the name of the enemy
He shall be appointed secretary to the time spirit.
If he is giddy—if everywhere he sees the staircase leading down—
Let him put out his hands.

Brother, we will uphold you—
Here are the sources of your courage:
In this miner limping
This blinded soldier
(Something redder than poppies)
This negress bowed with cotton
The salesgirl from the five and ten
The Jewish professor from Leipzig
The young history teacher from Passaic
(She thought she was really supposed to teach history)
The Ethiopian shepherd with no flocks
The Chinese orphan whose mother lies under the house—
A city will be born of us and we will not desert you.

A man will not be giddy if he is not alone.
If you have heard the dawn-bird singing of tomorrow
You are not alone.
We who have built all foundations hitherto
Leaving you the elegant labors of the superstructure
Where you sit spinning chimeras—
We are on the march to build that city here—
One-armed, one-legged, hungry and defrauded;
Overworked, militant, gathering strength—
Now we are going to share with you.
You shall have a share of healthy digging
And we will show you how to build a look-out tower that will not
    sway in the wind.

ANTIDOTE

A freight-car philosopher came to my front door saying
Madam
For all I know you may have found a way of life
But is it adequate and how far does it carry you?
Can it compensate for the heartbreaks and the hardships
For the landlord's birthday faithfully recurring
For the no-chicken in the pot and no-cookies in the cupboard
For the shoes with paper soles and the soul without wings?
(Meanwhile a hundred thousand Somalis tramping through the mud
Scabbing on their neighbors to no good end.)
Can you bear it, madam,
Can you absorb the big hurts along with the little ones?
Do you know that the Chinese wall protecting the Rosenberg family
Is full of holes and all the contradictions of capitalism
Come pouring through to carry you off?

Yes madam he said, dunking the dry bread in the coffee,
You are lucky to have a roof to your mouth.
Any day now the sky will be solid silver with the enemy fleet
And then where are you?
Ostriching in the cyclone cellar maybe.

We have no more lullabies, madam.
The records are all broken.
I am selling a very superior tonic for the nerves however
A definite antidote for poisoned thinking
A cure for chronic contemplation of the navel
Night fears and loss of self-respect;
The only known restorative of vigor—
A red card entitling you to membership in the human race.

IV. Hope

Steel bones will hold
And concrete flesh will cling.
The monster's roots clutch deep Manhattan schist.
They built better prisons once;
Beauvais and Chartres trap the amplest soul—
But here—this bare-faced box announces:
You have sold your youth
Your days of beauty belong to Standard Oil.

You feed the filing cabinet—
It is no use.
Stuff one to bursting—his brother comes up ravenous.
The gulls are wheeling in the bay
The boat is off for Alexandria.
(Who feeds the engines? Clearly not the passengers—
They can barely wipe their own noses
And surely, oh surely, they can not cut their toe nails.)
The filing cabinet has had his lunch—
You have half an hour by the window.
Forego the peanut butter sandwich—
We must reconstruct the city.
Leave one monster for a monument—
A tower of Babel to remind us of confusion.
(Why must seven million apes and angels dance on one tiny point of
     land?
Can you dance the Seventh Symphony in a night club?)
The Elysian fields are just around the corner
The lyre of Orpheus faintly sounds above the taxi horns;
Mingled with the steel bouquet of the subway
We smell the purple flowers of Hades.
The news stands sell six pomegranate seeds in a cellophane bag
And the ferry on the Hudson-Styx will carry you for an obol.
Nothing is lacking to modernize the picture
Except one large airplane carrying packages of greenish gas.

Olympus too is ravished
And Valhalla, but if Thor
And Wodin plod in chains behind the crooked cross
And Zeus stands stiff-armed in that dread salute
Shall we, the children of Prometheus, permit the rape?

Or shall we in our hordes
Swarm up the mountain and release our friends?
Behold! Dionysos shall carry the red banner
Erda shall walk the picket line
While Freya and Persephone bring joy to the strikers.

Then forward immortals!
Earn your resurrection on the barricades
And join with us to build a new Valhalla;
The world is ours—we can not spare one flower for our foes.

They of the golden touch
Let them eat their golden herring.
A tight horizon may be gold as well as iron;
Cellini and the Inca craftsmen and your dentist
Let them keep the gold.

Neighbor!
Are we dogs or dowager duchesses
To sit so stiffly across the car?
Twenty minutes is a long time to be confronted with a face
Wearing the curtain marked ASBESTOS.

For we are all hung from the same hook.
If the train should stall here under the river
And nothing come out of the tunnel but smoke—
Well—it happens today instead of tomorrow
But some of us haven't squared our accounts
And none of us will make the promised land.

So why not anticipate the end of capitalism
And spare each other a pleasant smile?
You talk such nonsense, Mr. Hitler.
Anyone can see the human race is all one family
And needs to cultivate its garden.

A skyscraper has malicious mineral magnetism
Grins at us with square stone teeth
Gobbles us
Throws us up and down fifty stories
Digests us thoroughly
Ejects an indistinguishable brownish mass.

A little house digs its toes deep in the ground;
It is a motherly hen and will not bite
Like these death-eyed dinosaurs.
(Men shaken from the carapace
Assimilated to zero in the maw.)

Very soon
I think we shall not need so many filing cabinets.

FOURTH INTERMEZZO

LET MY PEOPLE GO

Pharaoh on his purple carpet
Never knew who rowed his boat
Never noticed if a slave slipped his ankle chains
By dying at the oar.

We called on Pharaoh in his office this morning
To arbitrate the speed-up.
There it was, the same old carpet
Thicker, if anything.
The slave with the feather fan was absent

(Courtesy of General Electric)
And we weren't clanking our ankle chains—
Not much.

Mr. Pharaoh, we said,
We've had enough of your phoney arbitration—
This is a strike.

This afternoon outside the gates
I saw Moses smite the overseer.
You see it was this way, Your Honor—
He was defending a fellow-worker—
The overseer was armed.

Comrades and fellow-workers
Up to a certain point Moses has been our leader
But he started something he can't finish.
Ever since he apologized for striking the rock
He's lost his grip.

Here, one of you fellows—
Plant a tree or something in memoriam—
We have to hurry to the promised land.

V. ACT SWIFTLY

It is not true that all mankind lives in caves
Watching fire-shadows on the walls
And that only the philosophers will lead us out.
Did Plato forget something?
Did he forget who feeds the philosophers?

He knew that a few men grabbed the best seats in the cave
While the others carry them piggy-back;
Only the riders can watch the movies—
The others are bent under burdens
Or on their knees digging.

The philosopher has been standing and pointing outward
Since four-sixty B.C.—
There will be no exodus from the cave
While the armed servants of the piggy-back riders
Stand at the opening and say No.
You diggers and carriers pass the word along
Stand up and stretch!
Leave the riders sitting on the cold floor
Rush the guards—
It must be nice outside!

Fifth Intermezzo

Render Unto Caesar

An order has gone forth abrogating all the old miracles.
The new miracle is as follows:
Upon a day the sun begat a sun-god
Or the thunderer begat a thunder-bird
Or a pack of wolves were begotten on the wolf of Romulus—
Something begat something, that is clear;
The rest is delphic, orphic, eleusinian.

Behold the Begat!
Hail the Begat!
When thou sittest in the beer parlor
Risest from thy bed
Let thy greeting be
Hail Begat!

Great is the Begat
He hath created Aryans in his own image:
Slant-eyed Aryans
Moorish Aryans
Aryans from Somaliland.
Great is the Begat.

Merciful is the Begat.
Empires and dynasties were paralyzed and falling—
He hath glued them together a little.
Who would not give two quarts of blood
To keep the rulers ruling a little longer?

A little longer, oh great and merciful Begat,
A little longer, miraculous impossible Begat,
Time is a virgin that hath conceived one more miracle
And we shall see what we shall see.

Coda

These are the invocations against spastic paralysis of the horizon:
REMEMBER
That the beauty of the past is seen in amber
And the beauty of the future is a fresh fountain;
That tomorrow is the judgment day
And you will be needed in court.
BELIEVE
That you will not totter—you will be upheld
By the warm friendly arms of the workers around you
And the memories of those who will not see what they have built.
HOPE
That presently our credentials will only read:
"Genus homo, habitat—earth."
In the name of Jesus, St. Francis and Bartolomeo Vanzetti,
Is not that enough?
ACT SWIFTLY
Seize the mischief makers by the shoulder
By the neck.
(Useless to box them up.
Kindness to cobras is an expensive virtue
And from beer-hall to Berchtesgade is not far enough.)

Afterward
When the iron ring is melted
And the golden ring is returned to the Rhine maidens
On that day when man is master of the wheel
And not of another man
When the howitzers rust in museums
And only the painter will question the color of a face
On that day
With all flags flying
To celebrate the birthday of the human race
Then kindness will cost no more than sunshine.
Meanwhile one-third of the nation can not afford it
Meanwhile the ink flows in an angry river.

The embers of the old Valhalla
Paint the sky with orange blood and fiery smoke;
But the long fingers of the morning are reaching out behind the clouds—
You can only improvise where the parts have not been written
And keep the horizon open for the dawn.

"The Price of Liberty" first appeared in its entirety in Upward, now entitled Compass.

THE FLOOD

Mary Elizabeth Burtis

Ezra Adams came in from the barn,
A lantern swinging loosely from his hand.
His hair was wet, his shoulders bright with rain.
Thin muddy trickles ran across the floor
Beneath his heavy boots. He struck a match
Against the iron stove; then touched the wick,
And turned it to a point before he spoke.
"The river's rising still," was all he said
As he went out. His solid form soon blurred
Against the grayness of the sodden earth.
Rachel, his wife, stood at the window watching,
Until he dwindled to a small, dark point
With only motion left to mark the line
Between him and a world of sombre things—
Motion and a prick of lantern light
That drew a thin, bright arc against the gray.
She watched till he was gone; then pulled the shade,
And turned the center table lamp up high,
Slowly not to break the chimney glass.
"The river must be swollen bad," she said
Speaking to the old man in the chair
Before the stove, while he said after her
"Quite bad" as if the thought had been his own.
"It's not like Ezra not to say a word.
There were a heap of lanterns on the hill.
I guess the men are working at the dam.
Now, Grandpop, don't you fret Miss Ellis none,"
She cautioned as she heard a step outside.
"Don't say a word to her about the river.
I reckon she'll be thinking 'bout that man
Who's lying sick in Boston Hospital."

23

The door flew wide, then slammed behind a girl.
Rose Ellis looked at them with frightened eyes,
Heedless of the way the water dripped
In shiny puddles on the clean swept floor.
"The river's roaring so. I couldn't stay.
We heard it in the schoolhouse yard.
It sounds like thunder but it doesn't stop.
They say that men are tearing down the dam
Because the upper pond is flooded now."
"I reckon so," Rachel answered her.
"Ezra's gone up there. I wouldn't fret,
If I were you. Land sakes, it's rained before."
"It's rained before," the old man echoed her,
Rocking in his chair before the stove.
Rose Ellis threw her cap and coat aside.
"Where's Edna May?" she asked.
"I saw her leave the schoolhouse long ago."
"She'll be along before its suppertime.
Why don't you go and rest awhile, Miss Ellis?"
"I'm going to telephone to Ronald's folks."
"It ain't no use. The lines are broken down."
"Well then, I'll go to him. I've got to know.
He must be through the operation now."
"He'll be all right, Miss Ellis, just you wait—
You said he always was a strong young man—
And I'm afraid the train won't run to-night."
"Won't run; what do you mean, won't run?"
"The twelve o'clock got stopped above the cut.
They had to take the people off in boats
And bring them down into the town to stay.
There won't be trains for quite awhile, I guess,
With half a mile or more of tracks washed out.
Now you'll just have to wait a day or so.
If news is bad, you'll hear it fast enough—

Good news won't spoil by keeping for a bit."
"I reckon you won't hear for quite a spell,"
The old man said so unexpectedly
It startled them. But when he spoke again
He mouthed his words and mumbled to himself.
"I mind the flood of '88 right well.
We lost a heap of stock and grain in that.
Before the dam the river used to run
Across the orchard land. It rose so high
That water sloshed about inside the barn.
There ain't no floods like that one now-a-days."
Rose Ellis looked at him, her eyes alarmed,
Her fingers twisting at her green wool skirt.
"The river couldn't flood like that again,"
Rachel said, "so don't you worry none—
Old Grandpop's living back in '88.
Why Ezra's over working at the dam.
They're going to tear it down and let her go.
There ain't no land that can be damaged much
Below the pond—only fields and woods."
She folded up her work and laid it down.
"Well now, I'll set the supper out for us
I reckon Ezra won't be in at all.
But here comes Edna May by all the noise."
A child wide eyed and eager came to them.
Her cheeks, round and bulgy like a squirrel's
With rows of tiny freckles flecking them,
Were pink and moist. Her voice was shrill with news.
"Oh Ma, they haven't any lights in town.
Mrs. Warren got out her old lamps.
She said down street there's candles in the stores."
"Land sakes", her mother said, "just think of that."
They talked excitedly about the storm
While Edna May set dishes on the table,

And Rachel browned potatoes on the stove
And put her beaten biscuits in to warm.
Rose Ellis walked about uneasily.
She lifted up a dish, then set it down.
She stooped to stroke the kitten on the hearth
But straightened up before she touched its fur.
She crossed the room to raise the window shade
And peer into the night across the hill,
Where lights were moving points against the dark.
She could not hear the voices of the men—
Only water roaring endlessly.
Rachel dished the food and set it down,
Then filled the stove again. The fire licked
The edges of the wood in crackling lines
That caught in flame with sudden glowing heat.
The drowsy kitten stretched himself and slept.
The lamplight drew a circle 'round the table
Soft and bright and holding shadows back.
But all the warmth and old security
Was not enough to keep the storm outside.
The swollen, angry river rushed headlong
In deep reverberations through the night
Until the quiet room was filled with sound.
Rose Ellis pushed her plate away untouched
And pressed her slender hands against her head.
"It's like being up too high," she said to them.
The old man looked up from the apple pie
That he was eating without the aid of teeth.
"It didn't rain like this in '88,"
He said. "I never saw it rain like this."
But soon he brought his thought back to the pie
Since food was all that held him to the present.
Edna May said nothing while she ate
But afterwards her tongue ran fast enough.

When Rachel cleared the table things away,
They drew their chairs about the kitchen stove—
Rose Ellis talking restlessly to them,
Rachel sewing at her patchwork quilt,
The old man sleeping in his rocking chair
And Edna May curled snugly on the hearth,
Sometimes looking at a picture book,
More often playing with her Muggens cat.
Impinged upon the deeper sounding flood
Of waters roaring heedless through the night
The quiet noises in the room held both
Conjunction with the sum of sound
And yet a fine identity of self
Just as a man among a milling mob
Both to himself and those who are with him
Maintains Selfhood against the pressing men.
The clock ticked on; the kitten purred content;
The old man's breath was broken in his sleep.
Before they were aware of Ezra's step,
The door flung wide and he was in the room.
Wind and rain swept by him from the storm.
The lamp flame lengthened to a thread of sparks,
Trembled, steadied, broadened back to light.
High, thin shadows leapt up on the wall
Then dropped and merged into the solid form
Of Rachel standing upright in the room,
Her sewing scattered on the wooden floor.
She waited, taut with fear, motionless.
Rose Ellis whispered "Ronald" only once
And waited, staring at the man's set face.
Edna May's wide eyes grew wider still.
The old man yawned. The clock ticked quietly.
Ezra set his lamp down on the table.
"The river's broken loose," he said.

"While we tore down the dam to let her go
The water forced a way out under ground.
It's running where the old bed used to be
Across the orchard and behind the barn.
I let the stock go. They'll find a way
To save themselves. The barn's gone almost out."
"Is it as bad as that?" Rachel asked.
"Worse," he said and crossed the room to her.
"It's hell broke loose out there. We've got to go.
It won't be safe to stay here in the night."
"I guess the Scotts will let us sleep with them,
If we must go. I'm not afraid to stay."
"We won't sleep at the Scott's to-night.
The river will be up to them by dawn.
I tell you, Rachel, it's no little flood.
It's not just water sloshing in the barn.
The river's eating out the solid ground.
Nothing can stand. This house will go and Scott's.
Get heavy blankets and a lot of food.
We're going up on the hill tonight to stay.
The road to town is lost in roiling mud."
"This house will go," she whispered after him,
White-lipped, her eyes dark shadows in her face.
"Don't stand and look at me like that," he said.
"I'm going to get some papers from the safe.
Miss Ellis, gather up what you most want,
But don't take much. Help Rachel with the food
And things to keep us warm up on the hill."
They heard him fumbling with the metal knob
And pulling at the heavy iron door.
Rachel drew her hand across her eyes,
Her shoulders straightened up, her hands unclenched.
She walked swiftly to the cellar door
And wrenched it wide. "Land sakes," she said,

"Come here, Miss Ellis. Look at what's down there."
Below her, water washed against the stairs.
A thin wave touched the fifth step from the top,
Broke, slipped back, and reached the stair again.
Vegetables and wood and pickle jars
Bobbed up and down, moving with the flood.
She shut the door. "Let them lie," she said
"There's nothing that we really need to-night."
Once roused she worked as one who knows the need
Of driving thought and body in a task
Where time gnaws into action steadily.
She piled up blankets on the kitchen table,
Filled a basket high with bread and meat,
Bundled Edna May into her coat,
Leggings, scarf and scarlet woolen hat.
She got out Grandpop's heavy coat and shoes
But he had left the room. She called to him.
He came back dazedly, his face disturbed.
"My medal, where is it?" he said to her,
"The solid gold one Grant himself pinned on?"
She got him in his coat and tied his scarf.
"I guess your medal's in the safe," she said.
Ezra and Rose Ellis came back then.
"I've got your wedding necklace and the ring
That mother left for Edna May," he said.
"My medal, Ezra, have you got that too?"
"I didn't see it, Grandpop. It's not there.
You must have put it down somewhere yourself."
The old man shook his head. "I can't find it"—
His voice was querulous, like a fretful child's.
"We haven't time to hunt for it, Grandpop,
Besides a medal isn't much to lose."
Ezra gathered blankets in his arms;
Rachel took the basket in one hand,

The other held on tight to Edna May,
Who clasped her Muggens cat against her breast.
Rose Ellis carried blankets and a bag
Which she had stuffed with all her cherished things.
Ezra stopped and bent to turn the lamp;
Rachel looked across the warm, bright room.
She bit her lip and turned her eyes away,
"All right, Ezra, blow it out," she called.

Outside the water lapped against their feet.
Its constant roaring followed all their steps.
Ezra swung the lantern back and forth
To light the roughness of the steep up-path.
The hill that had seemed friendly in the day
Became in darkness vast and alien,
A brooding mountain, deep with mystery.
Half way up they found a place
Sheltered from the wind by heavy trees.
Wrapped in blankets, they sat down to rest.
The lantern's curl of flame set in their midst
Drew them within a slender ring of light.
The old man dozed, waked and dozed again.
Edna May, her head in Rachel's lap,
Her kitten in her arms, slept rosily.

Sometime in the night the wind died down;
The cold rain stopped. The dark and sullen day,
With tears still on her cheek, first touched the sky
Beyond the eastern hills with a gray band
That was but little lighter than the night.
The darkness slowly sank into the hills
That seemed to draw the dying night to them,
So that against the dull glow of the light
They still raised up their solemn heads of black.

With the returning day, the valley stirred
And looked upon itself with aching eyes.
Its lovely green was marred by angry floods,
A yawning chasm driven through its heart—
Houses, farms, orchards, crumbled down,
Swept in a swirling mass of twisted things
Across the fields. Nothing of them remained.
Rachel, looking from a clearing, wept.
They walked along the high ridge of the hill
Until they struck a road that led to town.
Already smoke was rising from the streets
And all about there was excited stir.
Each house had opened wide its doors to those
Who came in from the hills, homeless, cold,
Sick with the weight of bitter emptiness
As years were swept away in one brief night.
They made a little world among themselves,
Remote and lonely as the farthest star
That, lost forever from the warming sun,
Can only light its way with its pale gleam.

But they did not depend on other worlds
Nor on the greater power of a sun.
Their work was touched with fierceness and with pride.
The men who wielded spades against the earth
Or bartered goods behind a wooden counter
Began to build the road-bed up and lay the tracks,
Follow the broken, twisted lines of light,
Dig out the roads, rebuild a bridge
And send their feelers to the outer world.
The younger women shared the hardest work.
Rachel followed Ezra on the tracks
Forgetting, in the pain of heavy task
And surging eagerness that caught all men

And bound them close to serve a common end,
The loss that had befallen them alone.
Rose Ellis wouldn't leave the house at first
But sat before the radio to wait.
"Some word will come to me from him," she said.
But when no word had come for many hours
She told old Grandpop he should listen now.
"You call me if you hear my name," she said,
My name, or his—Rose Ellis, Ronald Hedge.
And promise me that you won't go to sleep."
He promised her. "No, I won't go to sleep.
I'll try to think out where I put my medal."

By afternoon the sky was soft and blue.
Rachel and Ezra stood on their own land
And looked far down into the barren gash
That split the green earth open to the heart.
Houses had been there, flowering fields,
Age-old, sturdy trees. Nothing remained.
The slanting sun struck out a sudden fire
From something lying loosely in the sand.
Ezra made his way down carefully
And picked it up. "Why look—it's Grandpop's medal—
Ezra Adams, eighteen sixty-three."
He slowly climbed again to solid ground
And laid the bit of gold in Rachel's hand.
Her roughened fingers slowly closed on it.
Her eyes, tear-wet and brave, were raised to his.
"I'm glad," she said. "It's all that he had left."

RADIO AT NIGHT

Mildred Cousens

Now is the time that the dark flows in from the wide Atlantic,
The edge of the shadow glides over the miles of land,
Covering the restless continent far to its western beaches
With the peace of the homecoming hour and the stillness of night.

Then over the hemisphere listening there in the darkness,
The voices, the many voices, hover like birds in the air
That dip to earthward and rising, flutter and disappear.

The threads are tangled, the threads of sound, the golden music,
But over the lighted cities and towns where men are waiting
The words come clear as the clangor of bells.

The magic sound drifts over the Appalachian ridges—
Over the broad lakes held in the cupped hands of the hills,
Over the mighty rivers rushing along their valleys—
Out in the far Dakotas the tired man hitches his rocker
Across the faded carpet close to the dial—

Then lost, lost in the snows of the Rockies the voices,
Like ice-clad planes they are lost—only the strains of music
Schubert and Strauss and the wraiths of the women dancing
Swirl in the storm on the mountain-peaks of the Rockies—

There on the coasts where all day long the sunlight glistened
The dark lies now, and the voices drift out over
The pale white crescents that gleam like thin young moons—
The songs and the dances, the news of the day and the speeches,
The voice of the suave announcer, the sound of the gong—
Twelve o'clock by Pacific time—back in New York
The music is thinning a little, but way out in Frisco
The fun is beginning, the wine just starting to flow.

The voices float out over the western ocean
And are lost like birds in the deep fog of the dark.

"Radio at Night" first appeared in *The Saturday Review of Literature.*

Bread Loaf Pass

THE ELLS

Kile Crook

New England houses never were designed:
On foursquare rock foundations, they occurred.
Not so much raised by hands as by a mind,
On sills as sternly adzed as Calvin's Word,
They formed in sharp rectangularity.
And they were homes for men. And there they stood
Unbudging, like the men's theology;
Like it,—complete, unbeautiful and good.

Time warped the weather boards and cramped a creed:
Men wanted ampler room, less sulphurous hells.
Old houses grew more spacious at their need
With strictness mellowed by haphazard ells,
(A lean-to jutting here, a new wing there,)
Illogical as mercy, and as fair.

"The Ells" first appeared in the New York *Times*.

FANTASIA ON THE SHEEPSCOT

Christine Turner Curtis

I.

The day took tone from a gentian blue
Of crinkles that the mild wind drew
On the pale shell of Sheepscot—
Where we walked
The tide exuberant had chalked
A ribbon on the rusted reeds—
Had bound with salt a blackened skiff,
And in the resinous air, a whiff
Of ocean swam from the spear of bay.
Across our way
We saw gold caterpillars tack,
And others, furred in ginger and black,
Seemed striped as if to state,—life tends
To be at the centre, bright: dark on the ends.

II.

"But this is no moment, in this trenchant air
To gnaw the wafer of despair
That makes so wry a diet
When the soul plumbs its quiet."
I said, "Come, gallant friends,
As into cobalt air the road ascends,
And our good truncheons tap
The hard-spanked ruts, or prick the nap
Of mosses, clip rock shoulders gray,
Let us be married to this arrogant day,—
With trees exchange
Ichor for ichor, become wild, strange;
Entwined with bramble, fused with grove,
And that cloud bank that pours from puce to mauve!"

III.

A knuckle of road that leads
To the unexplored,—the walker needs
No other spur; on such he whets
The steel of his resolve; he nets
Potent response: a cinnamon dusk
Under black pines; a rusk
Of ridge that slants to the mowing land,
Where silver eddies hoop the tanned
Islands, and the long-billed snipes
Whistle; where tidewater stripes
The marshes, and a bluebell creek
Attempts to sleek
The harsh hair of the meadowgrass,—
And ferries clouds like slush in its flowing glass.

IV.

We passed a lily pond, a knoll
With spicy stole
Of juniper; there on the ledge
Where river wind was buffed by a hedge
Of mustard cedars:—dark and square,
A mansion sat with a regal air.
Under the weathered eaves a rim
Of beading made a fretted trim.
A passing driver stopped his team
Of glossy Percherons; a gleam
Shot from his eye, "That house is waitin' yet,
For the French queen, M'rie Anto'nette!"
"We know," we cried, "we've heard the tale.
She lost her head on the eve of setting sail."

V.

But a tramper has his queer
Imaginings: the house looked drear

37

For that bejeweled queen—
To see snow on the flats, then green
Ice in the river; hear from her bed
The ponderous tread
Of winter, manacled with frost—
The valley roaring like a lost
Soul in the gale from the East
That gnaws like a ravening beast
The coast of Maine! It is possible she
Might have preferred to die across the sea.
The knife at the lovely nape
Might well have been her passionate choice of escape.

VI.

For every straitened heart
Takes its own pulse; savors the smart
Of our seclusion in the dark; our rue.
Even this Persian-blue
Petunia morning that depends
From the high stem of Heaven, rends
By its indifference; we are snared
In a perpetual prison! Down we fared
Through lanes of broom; the slope
Gave on a tiny graveyard, offering scope
For rumination; peace was throned
On the low markers; black bees droned,
And with chipped headstone for a back,
One leaned and smoked, his head upon his pack.

VII.

And so at languorous ease, one heard
A dark blue music, not of bird
Or river, with a fall
Like bittersweet that sprays a wall.

It ran in bubbles from the sills
Of hemlock woods, and sluiced the hills
With indigo—the grass was wool
That airy fingers card and pull.
The little knolls of Sheepscot clasped
The enamelled water; beech-leaves rasped,
And the oak boughs, agape,
Wore garnet like a toreador's cape.
Fall sunlight with a cymbal clash
Polished the gemlike tide and made it flash.

VIII.

In the fawn marshes never a reed
Moved, or a sedge let fall a seed.
Clamped in a vise of blue
Crystalline light, they drew
Their rigid ranks: each might have been
Wired with a silver pin.
A rising bluff
Put out the village: the mail cuff
Of graveyard fence encircled us about.
No stir there was to flout
The harmony; only under the roots,
Cicadas marshalling recruits
To twang the summer out in pings
Of low-plucked lutes and pizzicato strings.

IX.

But so at ease, the eye was sure to fall
On some sly cartpath, with a wall
That cantered teasingly beside,—it could
Lead us to Heaven, we thought,—at least a wood.
We'd take the chance at any rate,
Not hesitate.

It had a disappearing air, that wily chap
Of road not on the map.
Through dust as soft as plush
We loitered,—bushes made a hush
Of cloisters, and a tall roodscreen
Of gilded poplars hung a Byzantine
Embroidery,—there at the turn
A firtree made the lacework lighter burn.

X.

A twist to south,—long dusty grass
Whipped at our knees, and sassafras
Dangled its mittens dyed in apricot.
The long sky slot
Grew narrower: somber spruce
Darkened the hazels: a wood ruse
To hide those yawning cellar holes
And strangled apple boles
Where pioneers had gathered fruit, now dust.
The path made an upward thrust
And far down we could trace
The bridge like a tarnished lace
Spanning the Sheepscot; there Wiscasset flew
Its spires like lilies, creamy in the blue.

XI.

A rock, a cliff, a slab,
Scorched to the heat of blood, with a tab
Of lichen making antimacassar trim!
To lie, to hear the organ hymn
Of autumn woods, in counterpoint,
While oils of the sun annoint;
And moored to sky
As to a mother,—so to lie,

Lost in the indulgent light,
Locked in an inner sight,
Loosing identity in this tall dream
Cerulean,—a seam
Of granite under the hand, and at the lip
A checkerberry leaf or a balsam tip—

XII.

This is the best of life, the cream.
Now troubles seem
Spun out of spider gossamer:
Anxieties whir
Like lazy gnats in the sun.
The decades run
To yellow powder, like the flip
Of pollen on an arum's lip.
And as for love, its fever merges
Into the boughs' deep surges.
Once it was honey, wine and milk
To the palate; lustrous silk
To the senses; now remote and old,
It sighs itself away in the sun's dark gold.

XIII.

Gone now is cant; gone creeds and choirs.
Pale aspen pyres
Supply the tapers, firs the frankincense.
Pines render pastoral eloquence.
This is the moment to untwist
The tangled skeins of thought, to list
The good, the evil, and to solve
Present and future; to revolve
The tides of Empire in their mad
Precipitate careening—sad

How the mind sloughs it off, enrapt
In visions as by water lapped.
The limbs in ermine muffed
Cling to the rock like fern or a bluet tuft.

XIV.

"But come, my roisterers, my crew
Of hardy trampers, this won't do!
If by tonight we aim to reach the sea,
'Twill take some action of the knee.
All well to dream awhile,
But we are out to conquer the mile.
So, hearties, on with your shoes.
Up with the packs, we'll choose
The rearing, shifting main
With its blue chalcedony vein.
Before the sun takes flight
The notched bay should be in sight."
Three nubbly apples from a branch we tore,
And champing thirstily, took the trail once more.

XV.

That was a sly, a dwindling path, well mossed
At intervals: the dark boughs crossed
Above us: pine trees sang a dirge.
"Yet, courage, friends, soon we'll emerge
To upland pastures:—I allow
There stands the farmer with his spotted cow,
Who goggles open-mouthed to see
What manner of mortals we might be."
"My aunt" . . she tottered up the ridge,
So ancient, none of us could bridge
The distance in her faded eyes.
She cackled, raven-wise,

"Edgecomb's the town. I come a bride
To that there house; there too I like to'a died!"

XVI.

She pointed north; a runnel slid
Under a footbridge,—maidenly hid
By sugar maples on a dumpling hill
That Georgian house could soak its fill
Of sun, of dew, of sky,
And star-rain under the nebulae,
Like some tall Auvergnese tourelle
Where only ringdoves dwell.
"My husband sold when times was poor."
That snowy manor had a pure
Dignity that put to shame
Some humans one could name.
It had rich traffic with the clouds, the heads
Of trees and robins in their lofty beds.

XVII.

She croaked, "In that there place
I wished to breathe my last, on the lace
Of my own piller-slips: my daughters went
When the black pox was sent.
We pig it here, my brother's boy and me."
The hovel squatted under a shagbark tree.
A scrawny goat ran loose;
Red hens pecked near it, and a goose.
Old wagon wheels and a pile of silvered wood
Told where the barn had stood.
Around us corn stalks lisped and sighed.
Here life had sunk too low for pride.
A silence fell,—we lingered, caught
And chained as if by witches' spell to the spot.

XVIII.

The man, the cow, the woman stared us down.
We felt beneath the frown
Of three magicians who could read
Our secret lives, our hopes, our greed.
"I see you all before," the farmer spoke,
His gold tooth glinting, "Wa'n't you folk
Over Wiscasset way 'round stroke of nine?"
His long arm bound the corn with a leafy twine.
Smiling we owned it. The old crone
Fixed us with eye gouged deep in the bone.
Her skinny finger marked the rising ground:
Her dry lips moved without a sound.
Her look grew deep and sealed; it might
Commune with fate in a sibylline sight.

XIX.

"You foller yonder road." We turned
Back to the way we'd spurned.
The hill plunged up
From the valley's round teacup.
The farm was gone: the salt wind met
Our nostrils, acrid and wet.
The pike went loping down, a snaky thing
Green-polished as a grackle's wing.
Across the seaward galloping knolls
Blew yellow aspen scrolls.
The warm, the lazy path was lives away;
Another world, another day.
On salted gusts we saw our scarves outride.
Up went our collars: longer grew our stride.

XX.

There on the hilltop stood the village store.
The mistress peering through the door

Cried out, "No bus today, he can't be stopped
By hailin'." On the warm planks we dropped.
The wind went hurdling past; a brown
Old collie waddled down
The platform; crinkled an anxious nose,
Snuffled our packs, then curled himself to doze.
"Now Prince, come here,"
She called, "Don't be a bother, dear."
The door flew back, and out she stepped,
A tall and weathered dame who kept
A smile to rival a girl's—
The wrinkles framed it in a maze of swirls.

XXI.

She neared to chat; her apron smoothed,
Quick smiled and with her fingers soothed
Her dog, "Yes, I keep store:
Postmistress too, I am, what's more
Of Edgecomb." She'd a glance
Blue, puckish, with a lance
Of Yankee shrewdness; if unschooled,
She would not easily be fooled.
She tipped her head; there flowed
Together merriment and a code
Of courage,—flavor of quince,
So keen it made us wince
In sharp assent. It was a tartness flecked
With sweetness, found among the world's elect.

XXII.

"My throat is raw," I said, "as balm,
Frozos all 'round might work a charm!"
We bit into the cool: her dog pressed near
To scrutinize and peer,

And through his nose began to whine.
"Such an old baby, come, you lick off mine,"
She chuckled. "You would never b'lieve
All that dog knows, I'd grieve
To lose him as I would my hand.
He'd never leave me either, why, my land
They'd no more'n carried Captain out the house,
Prince, he crep' after me, quieter'n a mouse.
He clumb up to our bedroom, stair by stair,
A thing before he'd never even dare—

XXIII.

"He come; he set beside my bed.
All night he watched: seems 'sif he said,
'I'm here, don't fret,' and since that night
He never lets me outer his sight.
Seems 'sif he figgered it was left to him
To be the man,—you limb!"
She tucked his shaggy head beneath her arm:
She had a rare elusive charm.
She feigned to grit her teeth, "I vum
This dog is foolish as they come.
No better'n a beggar,—here, you take a bite."
The dog ran out his tongue in grave delight,
And every hair was eloquent
Of pride, of consequence and rich content.

XXIV.

A neighbor stopped for gas; with casual air
She held the nozzle, as if half aware.
She had a quip, a smile, "Of course you'll vote
Accordin' to reason." "If this aged boat
Hangs out to git us there, we'll win."
Glee filled her face. "The Lord won't count it sin,"

She flashed and kindled: back she came.
"That Frenchman on the hill, I name no name—
Wants him a liquor stand, up road a spell.
He knows I'm spank against him,—well
He hates me too, black-hearted frog;
He said he'd shoot my dog.
If so be he conspired
'Twould be the dearest shot he ever fired."

XXV.

In that bleak road we saw the beacon flare,
Challenge to tyrants everywhere;
Flicker of an eternal spark
Never entirely doused or dark.
We heard the dry leaves skirl.
A drop of rain fell like a smoky pearl.
"With all that drinkin' and carousin' near
'Twa'n't safe of nights,—that much was clear.
We're out to whip him; we shall do it too.
No, little girls, there ain't no mail for you."
The children lingered, "Have a look
In that warm sheltered crook
Of the shed; but mind the mother cat.
She'll claw at you 'sif you's a braided mat!"

XXVI.

A solemn boy behind big glasses stared
From the screen door: her quick smile flared,
"What you want, dear?
If candy, ice-cream or a ginger-beer,
You go and git it." He passed by
Swift as a rabbit, nibbling Esquimo pie.
He gave us all a quiet look
As if unwittingly he took

A childish stock. "That's my grandson.
You be good boy, dear. Now you better run
Or you'll be late to school." The glance he gave
Showed us that like the dog's, his role was grave.
"His father's sick to Boston, now his ma
Has gone to see him: Boston's pretty far!"

XXVII.

She looked away, a lantern in her face
Shone mellowly, "I ben here for a space
Of forty years, but I can't strain
Nor lift as once I did them bags of grain
Or chicken-feed, but then agen
Most folks would ruther die than keep a hen!"
She twinkled; stroked her dog's brown paw,
"Once Edgecomb township gits a law
Will set that rattlesnake to rights
Up road, I'll sleep again o' nights."
We rose to go: we said we deemed
The parting hard; she beamed.
"Come up next year—I hope you reach the coast
By bus or foot, whatever suits you most."

XXVIII.

"A queen," we said, "she could have been a queen!
That fearless heart, that flourishing green
Bay-tree of spirit, the adept
Delicate response that kept
Perfect alignment, the swift word
Light-footed as a fawn, and as unspurred."
Oh postmistress, the world is small,
And royal hearts are few; not all
The chilly neons of sky can quench
A kindled soul, or make it blench.

48

Though seeds and urchin shells
Shall stuff our knapsacks, schooner bells
And fog our heads,—a certain blaze
Lit up on Edgecomb shall transcend our days.

XXIX.

Down dropped the land to Boothbay, flank on flank,
The hills drew off; a lank
Cloud-dappled lowland smoothed and swelled.
The grass gave way, imperiously quelled
By ocean wind; fall butterflies,
Yellow as tansy under a rise
Of sandbank, sunned themselves at ease;
Fanning and fluttering; into the breeze
They seemed to bring
A thin Debussy theme, then cling
In knots of lemon-gold
To the land's fold,—
Till, sensing us, they took the air again
Light as the steeds that pulled Apollo's wain.

XXX.

Elixir of Maine tides that flow
Into the inlets, the salt bays, the low
Hillocks of fir; rich airs that sting
The blueberry leaves, and salt the seabird's wing—
They poured upon us strong ozone,
Bent down the roan
Cat-nine-tails in the swamp; blew flat
The stiff dust-coated goldenrod, and sat
Upon the willows; down they rode to earth.
With this baptism came new birth:
Sloughing of weariness, allay
Of old humiliation and dismay.

The East wind flung about us its ribbed tent
As down the Sheepscot towards the sea we went.

XXXI.

The sullen cloudbank drew its sad
Gray lid from west to east: we bade
Farewell to the gilded noon.
The seagulls in platoon
Screamed over; colors went.
Metallic green with the gray was blent.
The day was tinged with the mulled
Feeling of night; the edges dulled.
One tasted tincture of the fall
And afternoon, with its call
To tenderness, to brown
Study and thought. We hurried down
A land that grew intense and aware
Of the proud lordly element waiting there.

XXXII.

And then we heard dishevelled green
Water champ in the bay, between
Dark fir-trimmed promontories. Tossed
Into a turmoil, and unglossed,
It seemed to drive from Spain; the piers
Shambled and clanked like tethered steers,
And our charmed eyes as if long pent
Went rushing out to the rent
At the bay's head,—to the churning gray
Lumbering ocean, out and away
To rocking, tantalizing space;
To intermingle, to interlace
With fathomless and century-old
Marine horizons, challenging and cold.

XXXIII.

For we have ballast there,— the heart
Leaps to the distant and apart.
At visionary fonts we quench
Undying thirsts: we wrench
From mystery a nourishment
Palatable and exigent.
It is the miracle not plain
To read that satisfies, like rain
That pulls a silver stop
On every olive wave, to clop
In chords of crystal: it is not
Banners or drums or the hot
Breath of applause that hold us long,
But distance, blueness, sound of the sirens' song.

XXXIV.

Yet not where herded crowds abound
Are these intangibles to be found.
The delicate mainspring must be touched
In secret, never carelessly clutched.
So is released the exquisite shock
Of re-creation, that can unlock
The fettered powers. All life is clean,
Charged with electrical unseen
Currents, and Pentecost descends
Not in a common flash, but wends
To each one separately and alone;
To each in his own language and tone,
As a bud opens cherry-red or blue,
So life unfolds in its own tint and hue.

XXXV.

And Time, sweet Time, is the mother of all;
Resolving the small

Dissonances, mellowing the great
Sorrows. Time is fate.
The near at hand compels distrust.
Smeared with myopic must
The present towers to the top of the sky.
We see but with a termite's eye.
But Time is loving, godlike, mild,
Smoothing with undefiled
Hand that is cooling and pure.
It hollows the rock and tamps the moor:
It brings us all to fruit,
And tenderly returns us to our root.

XXXVI.

Envoy

We shall not come to Sheepscot side
For many moons:—snow druggets hide
The changeling waters, where they lick
Wiscasset shores; white steeples prick
Geranium sunsets, and the cold
Frost-stiffened spruces fold
In rabbit redingotes.
Snow mounds the river boats.
In those up-trundling emerald lanes
The blizzard drives with long white reins.
Sunk to the past, in the past dissolved
Are the old riddles, still unsolved.
The world clanks on: the lances gleam:
Only the river keeps its virginal dream.

REFUGEES

Donald Davidson

And if men ask you why you fled, and what,
Will you make answer, then? The age is not
Friendly to riddling, wants its discourse plain.
Its microphone, geared to the leaping clocks,
Tells all, loud-speaking, what will wax or wane,
Immediate and conclusive; flashes out
The dog's fanged answer to the dragging fox.
Will have its blood. Knows what it is about.

And this is riddling—or a cricket's cry.

It was red morning when the young men came
And saw, girdled with enemies, the flame
Swallowing the wreck where some had chosen to die.
Unrecognized, unknown, their weapons hid,
They sauntered there, unbid,
And in the desolate glare while stones cried out
Swore blood-feud from that day.
And now, a hardy few, in rocky ground,
Untaken and unwanted still they range.

Pleiad Lake

ECHOES

Wilfred E. Davison

The primal rhythm? The wind among the hills,
That in its mighty sweep man's spirit fills
With fearful awe no moon-calm ever stills?

Ancient that voice as mountain heights are old,
A voice no human speech, however bold,
Has ever yet the meaning told.

But older yet, timeless as mystery,
Unfathomed as the days that are to be,
The ceaseless rhythm of the ageless sea.

Only the stars are older, but the roar
Of light-surf breaking on that boundless shore
Where time and space and being are no more,
Where chaos and the void and endless night
Thrust back, impregnable in might,
The surging swells from out the seas of light—
That mighty voice no human ear has ever heard
Since day upon the depths of darkness stirred
Responsive to the fiat of the Word.

Yet can at times the listening soul
Catch faintly strains of one harmonic whole,
Tremendous orbic cadences that roll,
Majestic symphony, sublime and free,
Throbbing till time shall timeless be
The immortal rhythm of eternity.

FACE TO FACE

Wilfred E. Davison

Your face I shall not see again,
For dust will fall at last to dust,
To rise in other fleeting forms
Forever changing, as they must.

For life is but the moving force
That moulds the dust to transient shape,
But flows in endless impulse on
To make new forms, then to escape.

But I shall know that spirit then,
The soul that shone from out your eyes,
Half hidden by the fleeting form
Like stars when clouds drift through the skies.

Free from the dust and clouds of earth,
Your spirit shall forever shine;
And I shall know then face to face
What hidden here could not be mine.

For then the glass of darkness cleared,
We'll see with more than mortal sight;
What now in form is shrouded here
Will shine revealed in cloudless light.

MEMORIAL

Wilfred E. Davison

Give me no marble slab nor sculptured bronze
To keep a dead name living when my body dies.
Let all that was of passing worth go back to earth
Where all that's mortal lies.

My monument be what of living truth
Has flowed through me to other men.
So shall survive what is of lasting worth.
Thus though I die, then shall I live again.

TWELVE DAYS

Robert Allison Evans

(FOREWORD)

One bleak, rainy day in November, 1926, Black Creek broke through its dike at Tomhicken Mines, Pennsylvania, and poured millions of gallons of water down an old mine breach, into the workings below. The escaped torrent cut deep into the sandy till overlying the coal beds, washing thousands of cubic yards of surface material into the black slopes and gangways of the mine.

The day-shift miners were all at work when they heard the thunder of the inrushing flood. Throwing their tools aside, they rushed to the nearest openings and escaped to the outside. All, that is, except Andy and his companions who were entombed for twelve days, without food, drink, or light. The rescuers reached them on Thanksgiving Day—all, excepting Old Dutch. But that is Andy's story:

It was rainin hard when we come inside
And the wind blew fierce as the fans of hell,
Most of the fellows was wet to the hide,
Mean as a maggot and willin to tell
Bosses and big shots to jump in the ditch,
Callin each other a son-of-a-bitch,
Nice little playmates to work with.

It was squish, squish, squish on the gangway bed,
For a half a mile to the foreman's shack,
Gettin the smell of the guy up ahead,
Passin it on to the fellow in back,
Shiftin the tools when our shoulder got sore,
Cursin the luck when we slipped on the floor,
Peeved at the drippers above us.

58

You could see a ring on the carbide lamp,
Like the halo girdlin a rainy moon,
Always a sign when the creek's on a ramp,
Itchin to hand us a juicy harpoon;
Just as I said when we spoke to the boss,
Blackie is waitin to give it a toss,
Maybe my guess didn't hit it.

He was markin time on a dirty pad,
And his face was glum in the shanty light,
Andy, he said, things is lookin quite bad
Stay here a minute til I eat a bite,
Chasin the workins, I ain't had the chance,
Huntin that water crack led me a dance,
Don't tell me that it didn't.

There's a half a foot on the pump house floor
And it's raisin fast when I come from there,
Take Petrokubi and three fellows more,
Two from the track gang and one from the spare,
Hook up the volute and cut in the lines,
Maybe we'll need her if I know the signs,
Hurry now, get the boys started.

I decided fast on the men I'd pick,
And I started out to collect them in,
Porky and Chichi, the Kid and Big Nick,
Guys that can take it and stay with a grin,
Coal crackin devils, exceptin the Kid,
He's got more gray matter under his lid,
Kind of a buzzard at figures.

It was nine o'clock when we reached the slope,
And we took time out for to eat our piece,
Dutch heard us talkin and hollered for dope,
Yelled that the water was on the increase,
Way down below us, his light's like a spark,
Doin a ghost dance alone in the dark,
Pump-runnin's lonely as grave yards.

While the boys ate lunch, I climbed down to him
And described the plan for the extra pump,
Damn well we need it, he said, looking grim,
Chust now the water is up to my rump,
You and them loafers had better work quick,
Loafers, by Cheesus, you all make me sick.
Dutch had a great way of kiddin.

We were coupled up to the column pipe,
And all set to go when we heard a roar,
Never, by god, did I get such a gripe,
All I could do was to yell at the four,
Grab up your lunch pails and follow my light,
Take to the manway and keep me in sight,
Hell busted loose all around us.

We were just in time when the flood roared by,
With a thunderin boom and a deadly crash,
Snappin our heels with an unearthly cry,
Drownin our wits with its devilish lash,
Showin no mercy at all to old Dutch,
He had no chance to get out of its clutch,
God rest his soul at the tellin.

We went up the pitch like a frightened bat
And the Kid was sobbin to break his heart,
Seein that Dutch must be drowned like a rat,
Nobody with him to help take his part,
God only knows we had all we could do,
Keepin ahead of the foul smellin stew,
Chasin us higher each minute.

It's the Black Creek, boys, and she'll fill the works,
Til the water reaches the drainage grade
I know of only one way that us jerks
Ever can be in another parade
Out in the sunshine, unless it's our last,
Playin slow music and on the long fast,
Not very pleasant to think of.

There's an open breast on the lift above,
With a ladder built on the manway side,
Let's take a chance that the water won't shove
Up there ahead of us, I'll be the guide,
Follow behind me and step where I do,
This rock is slippy and covered with goo,
Watch that you don't take a tumble.

We must take our time til we reach the top,
Or we'll break our necks on the bloody pitch,
Give me a boost while I grab the next prop,
There now, be careful, I'll give you a hitch,
One at a time now, for Christ's sake, look out,
Nick you big bastard, stop shovin about,
You're not the only potato.

Here we are, my friends, as the fellow said,
Just a jump ahead of the hungry brute,
You fellows skin up the ladder ahead,
I'll stay down here and attempt to compute
How far the water is set to invade,
Maybe we're not high enough above grade,
Better to know it beforehand.

Have you got a watch? I can't make mine go,
I suppose it stopped when the works got wet,
Nobody got one, then how'll we know
How long we're in here, we're bound to forget,
Daylight and nighttime have only one name,
Here in the darkness, it's one and the same,
Wouldn't that give you a headache.

Well, the water's off, but the gangway's full,
So I guess we're safe where we're sittin now,
Stop shakin Kid, it's a cinch that we'll pull
Out of this pickle, I recollect how
Them guys at Forty was in for a week,
That was a honey compared to this squeak,
They was entombed by a cavein.

We are huddled up like a nest of pups,
And our clothes are wet and our tongues are dry,
All we can hear is the splash in the cups,
Catchin the drips for our water supply,
Feelin the dark like a blanket of doom,
Spread on a putrefied corpse in its tomb,
Drowsy, like misery makes you.

We are holdin on to our carbide stock,
On the chance that maybe we'll need some light,
Each of us knows that our lives is in hock,
All of us anxious to put up a fight,
Figurin some way to get ourselves out,
Long as there's health there is no room for doubt,
No use of cryin about it.

I was dreamin hard, when I felt a change,
Of the cross-cut air from the left to right,
That set me clear on a way to arrange
Records for countin each day and each night,
Air pulls at night time and draws in the day,
Pulls to the surface or settles away,
I mentioned nothin about it.

I arranged a plan to conceal a coal,
One for each time that the air was turned,
Kind of a personal pants pocket poll,
Showin the number of days we're interned,
Sort of a yardstick to measure our guts,
Some of the fellows is bound to go nuts,
Then's when we'll need information.

We had all agreed to go light on food,
That was in our cans when the trouble came,
Every last morsel was carefully chewed,
Huntin for crumbs in the dark was a game,
Even our coffee was taken in sips,
After the sulphur was found in the drips,
That was a bad break against us.

On the third day in, by my pocket gauge,
I was dozin like when I felt a stir,
Porky, I yelled, in a god-awful rage,
What were you doin just now, over there,
Answer me quick, or I'll tear out your heart,
Even at that threat, he tried to act smart,
Gulpin a mouthful of victuals.

I was scared to look at the dinner can,
But I soon found out that he swiped it clean,
He wouldn't talk about when he began
Stealin the rations, and then I got mean,
Porky, you pot-bellied son-of-a-bitch,
I've got a god damn good notion to pitch
You and your carcass to Hades.

If a single one of us starts to starve,
You can bet your life that you'll pay the price,
I'll be the first one to start in to carve,
That sugar belly of yours for a slice,
Don't think I'm kiddin, you double-faced thief,
We'll soon be cravin a piece of raw beef,
Then you will see that I mean it.

On the seventh day we are huddled tight,
Like a juicy bunch of red garden worms,
Huggin our guts in to couple them right—
That keeps the gas pains from givin you squirms,
Chichi gets up and moves off in the dark,
Damned if he didn't go out for a lark,
True as I'm tellin you, buddy.

These here Wops are hot, if you're askin me,
When they're kept away from their women folks,
Peppers and garlic is their recipe,
Dago red wine and a wheel full of spokes,
Chichi, I hollers, quit wastin your force,
Keep it for Tini, you stud-minded horse,
Imagine that kind of a makeup.

It is tough to starve, but the thirst is worse,
When you close your eyes, you begin to see,
Scuttles of nice foamy lager, and nurse
Visions of springs, that are gurglin with glee,
Even the drippers that fall from the roof,
Make you forget that you're not acid proof,
That's when you're headin for trouble.

As I tell the Kid, he must keep his head,
Or the fever's likely to get his goat,
One little swallow of that stuff, I said,
Shrivels the guts like a corduroy coat,
Jesus, he yells, can't you let me alone,
You mind your business and I'll mind my own,
Damned if I couldn't have crowned him.

I took off my shoe and sliced out the tongue,
And I cleaned the dirt the best that I could,
Even the fellow that has to be hung,
Gets what he wants before he wears the hood,
Leather is not what I'd pick for a meal,
Honest, the tongue tasted worse than the heel,
Not that I'm kickin about it.

The eleventh day, we was munchin shoes,
Like a flock of goats at the city dump,
No longer human, we're actin like screws,
Snappin and snarlin and ready to jump
Over the traces at any excuse,
Bitterly blamin our filthy abuse
Onto the pot-bellied big shots.

I could see our end and I didn't doubt,
That we'd find it soon if I lost control,
Hey, Petrokubi, you're stinkin us out,
Go to the gangway, you foul livin Pole,
That goes for all of you, I'm gettin sore,
I'll brain the next one that uses the floor,
This place is worse than a pig pen.

The Kid got up, with a crazy wail,
And he crawled away from our slimy cell,
Down on the gangway, we heard him unveil
All of our scandals and curse us to Hell,
Yellin defiance and then not a sound,
Quick as a mine rat, I sprang with a bound,
Too late to stop him from drinkin.

This mine water acts like a styptic bath,
If you take a drink on an empty gut,
Crampin the muscles that lie in its path,
Twistin the entrails and tyin them shut,
I know of only one way you can stop
Short of convulsions and that is to drop
Warm fluid into the belly.

66

I can see us yet as we struck a light,
As we stood by the side of the tortured boy,
Porky was eyein me up in his fright,
Guessin already that I might employ
His well-fed carcass, to get what I need,
Shakin for fear that he'd pay for his greed,
Big Nick and Chichi was willin.

I proposed to them that we save the Kid,
And I told them we'd need somebody's blood,
Grab that big porker and give him a skid,
Lay him down flat on his back in the mud,
Hold to him tight while I run for a cup,
Bash in his skull if he tries to get up,
I'll be around in a minute.

So I took a rope from a dinner can,
And prepared a noose for a tourniquet,
Porky starts yorkin when he saw my plan,
Turnin a color I'll never forget,
Faintin away as I opened a vein,
Nick held a cup as it started to drain,
Awe-struck for fear it was murder.

When the cup was full I applied the knot,
And it stopped the blood out of Porky's wrist,
Here, Chichi, help give this dose while it's hot,
Nick can look after that fat pessimist,
Pry up his teeth and look out he don't bite,
He needs a doctor to tend to him right,
Poor Kid, I think he's a goner.

It was nasty work to get him to drink,
But the blood was warm and it did the trick,
Shortly we noticed his cheeks gettin pink,
Then, when we saw that he wasn't so sick,
Back to the cross-cut, we lugged him with care,
Makin a bed with our coats for him, there,
Honest, I never felt colder.

We got Porky up, none the worse for wear,
But he's gone plain nuts from the awful strain,
Laughin and whinin and tearin his hair,
Weak as a baby but hard to restrain,
Now that we're tied up with two men to serve,
God knows it's tougher to keep up the nerve,
Some of us can't go much farther.

They was all asleep, as I sat on guard,
And I checked the days that we'd spent in here,
This is Thanksgivin, I said, thinkin hard,
I'll bet our women are crazy with fear,
Fear that the rescuers won't be in time,
Fear that we're buried in culm and slime,
They know the whole thing's a gamble.

For the women pay when their men get caught,
And they stick around til they know the worst,
Crowdin the mouth of the mine, so distraught,
They must be watched or they'll try to go first,
Not that their grief isn't honest or real,
Only they show it with more pep and zeal,
Sort of an old minin custom.

When the shift comes out, they all make a rush,
For the latest word from the rescuers,
Taking the bad news with kind of a hush,
Greetin the good news like wild rioters,
Sharin their troubles and sharin their fears,
Comrades in action and comrades in tears,
Honest to goodness devotion.

I should rub the Kid, but I'm too damn weak,
I begin to fear that the jig is up,
Porky is rollin his eyes like a freak,
Chichi just whines like a seven day pup,
Maybe I made a mistake from the first,
Dutch didn't suffer this devilish thirst,
He went out quick, like a soldier.

I was so played out, that my mind went blank,
And I had a dream that I heard a call,
Andy, hey Andy, it rose and it sank,
Andy, hey Andy, it kept up a bawl,
Andy, hey Andy, hey Andy, it's me,
Andy, hey big boy, the gangway is free,
Why in the hell don't you answer?

Well it's still a dream when it comes to that,
For they found us sick as a crowd can be,
Cooped in a hole that a sensible rat
Wouldn't be found in, and stated that we
Couldn't have lasted another two days.
Maybe the Boss of the underground ways,
Planned a Thanksgivin Day for us.

LETTER TO THOMAS WOLFE

Kimball Flaccus

The angel on the porch is poised in stone,
With marble features calm, unscarred by lust,
Fixed in perpetual grace,
While your familiar face,
Once mobile and alive, is turned to dust.
Are you still lost, alone?
Is your wild heart at rest,
Or by each changing mood caught and oppressed?
You were a boisterous comrade when the sky
Reeled with a blaze of stars;
When roused to anger you out-swaggered Mars.
You slaved and brought prodigious books to birth;
Restless, and strangely shy,
And overcome by hurricanes of mirth,
You ranged through time and over sea and land.
Inscrutable and dumb,
With brooding eyes, and pointed chin in hand,
You dreamed of moments passed and years to come.

As sparrows, terrified, with nervous talk
Chatter at length
And deprecate their enemy the hawk,
So did the impotent ones lament your strength;
As minnows fear the trout
That lunges at white water, swift and free,
Fighting his fierce way upward from the sea,
So the embittered critics, dolt and lout,
Safe in the shallows, scorned your perilous course,
Envied your driving force
In currents where they never ventured out.

70

Well I remember walks with you at dawn
Through city streets, your great impatient stride,
Your sullen, furious glances that defied
The armed, brass-buttoned guard
Who laid his truncheon hard
Against the feet of cold and sleeping men.
You shook with passion and your lips were drawn,
Your banner in that moment was unfurled,
Your brave impatient lance was raised in pride
To strike and strike again
The casques of all the tyrants in the world.

Where you have gone, old friend,
May there be meat and drink,
High-hearted talk, and laughter without end,
And mountains of blank paper, lakes of ink,
And girls so beautiful and grave and wise
That you will spend long nights in trying to link
Words in such patterns as will best reveal
The depth of violet eyes,
The curve of slender wrist,
The look of loneliness, the sweet surprise,
The body pulsing and the smooth throat kissed.

May you be happy, hearing
The rolling curses of the sons of toil,
The voice of thunder in the sharp recoil
Of axe on hard-wood in the upland clearing,
The cries of women in pre-destined pain,
The crash of wave on rock,
The soothing patter of rain,
The irrevocable shock
Of a gun fired, the sounds
That birds make,

The rustle of a snake,
The querulous speech of hounds.
Over gigantic cities may you feel
The clash of vibrant steel,
The hum of dynamos that hour by hour
Sit hunched like norns and spin their rune of power.
And may you be aware
When apple orchards bring
Sweetness into the air,
Ripeness into the bin,
Cider into the barrels of charred oak.
May you be still acquainted
With brush fires that on blue October days
In mountain pastures raise,
Gracefully-curled and thin,
Their tantalizing pyramids of smoke,
When maples are transmuted, color-tainted,
And frost sinks deep,
And the whole earth prepares itself for sleep.

You brought to living the unspoiled delight
That a child feels when turning
New corners in the realms of sense and sight,
Joyfully learning
The qualities that sharp experience brings,
The sounds, the colors and the tastes of things,
Their roundness and their weight,
Their depth and shallowness, their tensile clutch,
Breadth, width, and touch,
Their fixed or tenuous or floating state.
And now, before your time,
With steep hills yet to climb,
So many yielding women yet unclasped,
So many cities and lands

Beyond the unfathomed green,
So many honest hands
Of clear-eyed friends ungrasped,
Such wonder still unseen,
In spite of prayers, in spite of all the deft
And desperate maneuvres of the knife,
You have been reft
From the quick halls of life;
And whether the dim spark
Within your brain burned low
And sputtered out
Before you were accustomed to the dark,
While I still live I shall not know.
But I no longer grieve,
Who choose now to believe
Beyond the shadow of a doubt
That in your agony, grim and heroic,
You clung to life until
That brave gift was denied,
Then, like a stoic,
You faced the wall and died.
Mysteriously the spark was fanned,
Began to glow and waver and expand
Until it blazed up like a resinous torch,
Unseen by your attendants, but so clear
To your perception that it drove out fear,
Spilled glory on the angel on the porch,
On vanished ages cast its candid beam,
And lighted up new paths that lie ahead,
The territory of perpetual dream,
For you, Tom Wolfe, and all the adventurous dead.

Tamworth, New Hampshire, September, 1938

"Letter to Thomas Wolfe" first appeared in *Scholastic.*

DANCE OF DEATH

Kimball Flaccus

Most pines that fight their way to upper light
  Grow tall and straight for ever and a day;
You might believe them dead in the near night
  Of forest gloom, so still they are, and grey,
So smooth and cold and hard and gummed with mastic.
  But if you blaze the trunk the sap will spurt,
The bark will curl, reluctant and elastic,
  As though the tree were conscious of its hurt;
And peering up, you see the plumes aloft,
  And looking down, you note that roots are firm.
Like anchor chains they sink into the soft
  Waves of the yielding moss, defy the worm.
Yet even pines, those regal martinets,
  Played false by pride of posture, know defeat
When icy gales advance with blustering threats
  And mark their prey. Though regiments entreat
Respite and mercy, when the storm is spent,
  The slain, like soldiers, lie on splintered sides;
On comrades lean the wounded, still unbent,
  Uprooted, angled sharp by aerial tides.
And when these die they hardly know themselves;
  The brittle wood is seasoned by the weather,
Decay creeps from the ground, the sharp worm delves,
  The pines dance on, the quick and dead together.

JONATHAN TYNG

Kimball Flaccus

"He sat himself down in the midst of his savage enemies, alone, in the wilderness, to defend his home."—*History of Dunstable.*

Under black ice the Merrimac was sealed,
  The agile mouse transported to its nest
Grains of the corn that rustled in the field;
  The blind bear settled down to winter rest,
Rumor of snow to come was in the wind;
  At dusk the wild geese slipped across the moon,
But stranger news had spread, of white men pinned
  To trees by Indian tomahawks, and soon
This little town carved from the trackless waste
  Was empty as a city of the dead,
For the brave citizens, in nervous haste,
  Shouldered their guns, summoned their wives, and fled.
But one man at a window stood alone,
  In silence watched his neighbors out of sight,
Then, smiling, though his heart was like a stone,
  Kindled a crackling blaze against the night.

Bread Loaf

YOUNG FARMER

Robert Francis

One glance at him and you can tell
His fruit is clean, his corn is tall,
His sheep and cattle pastured well,
His buildings trim: house, barn, and wall.

You know the seed he sows is sound
As seed his forefathers have sown.
And when he ploughs and plants the ground
The crop must grow as he has grown.

"Young Farmer" first appeared in the *Christian Science Monitor*.

SPICEBUSH AND WITCH-HAZEL

Robert Francis

Spicebush almost the first dark twig to flower
In April woods, witch-hazel last of all—
Six months from flower of spring to flower of fall—
The alpha and omega if you please.
Yet how alike in color, setting, form:
Both blossoms yellow to confirm the sun,
Both borne on bushes that are nearly trees,
Both small and close to twig to keep them warm.
Only the learned might elucidate
Why one blooms early and one blooms so late.
Only the wise could tell the wiser one.

"Spicebush and Witch-hazel" first appeared in the New York *Times*.

THE THIEF

Robert Francis

Now night the sneak thief comes
Warily from the woods,
Shadowing our homes,
Greedy for all our goods.

Doors cannot keep him out.
Windows are for his peeping.
Soon he will roam about
In rooms where we are sleeping.

Who knows what he will take?
What he will leave behind?
Who knows when we awake
What we shall never find?

"The Thief" first appeared in *Voices*.

FIELD-WITH-A-STAR

By Frances Frost

There was a field
lay straight, not slanted.
For Spring on Spring
it had gone unplanted.
It sowed itself
with mustard and clover,
and chickory climbed there
Summer and Summer.

For twenty-three Junes
they'd come there solemn
and sat on a log.
His throat was a column
of wrinkled bronze,
her few words crumbled,
and each looked away
when the other stumbled.

This night they sat
like separate sages
as they'd sat for years
and would sit for ages . . .
lovers of love
without love's bother—
she on one end,
he on the other.

But sudden the sky
let go of glory;
there was no time
to breathe or be sorry.

The star fell smack
from the depths of heaven:
its heart was green
and its tails were seven.

It blew up the furthest
stump-fence, shook them
into the grass
and sight forsook them.
But he was a man
who, though briefly blinded,
was never a one
to turn feeble-minded.

He picked up himself
and bowed good-evening
and left the field
with its starry leavening.
She looked at the log
with no man to haunt it,
and nodded to God,
"Sort of pretty, wan't it?"

"Field-with-a-Star" first appeared in *The New Yorker*.

POEM FOR A YEAR'S END

Frances Frost

The leaves are buried now.
The world's leaves,
raw ochre, fire, the dusty plum, the purple,
the harsh bronze and the delicate flame, no longer
eloquent upon the vast autumnal
boughs, lie clenched with long rust under snow.

To the marked and unmarked graves the doomed bright leaves
drifted and perished; and the bones beneath
stirred not.
And the hurt mouths filled with bitter earth spoke not
of the hard remorseless wind or the empty branches.
Softly the white cloud lowered, and the dead
lie silently together under snow.

Drink now the cold and lucid air and call
no one man by his name,
but break the boughs of hemlock and of fir,
of pine and cedar, toss that living green
upon all burials.
Name no man's country, nor recall his face,
his hands, his voice, the way he had of walking.
the history of his breath.
But in the dark
over the white snow strew the shape of cedar
and choke the paltry words into your throat.

We who exacted blood and flesh and soul
of vanquished peoples, who are we to name
each in his secret heart the single love,
the several adored?

We who before a wounded world gave pledge,
who are we to take upon our tongues
the syllables of nations?
The promises are shattered and our honor
is a breath brief-visible in frozen air
and vanished on the unrelenting stars.

Year's end and our mortality are on us.
Break then the boughs, O doomed undead,
and let your heart be squeezed upon your blood
and let your throat be crushed upon its cry:
scatter the slow designs
against the white compassion of the snow.

And look not to the stars for comfort, dare
not lift your still face upward.
No sign is there;
in that huge ordered wilderness of worlds,
no hope.
The leaves are buried now,
the dead are crumbled.
Look to the earth and know it full and know
there will be room for all mortality
beneath the hushed forgiveness of the snow.
Stare then beneath the strewn boughs and the snow,
set eyes upon that final dark,
set eyes upon that peace:
speak no man's name.
It may be that the silent sky will curve
as a great wing bent down.

"Poem for a Year's End" first appeared in the New York *Post*.

JOSEPH BATTELL

Robert M. Gay

A happy man he must have been
With horses, mountains, and an inn,
Mile upon mile of his own trees,
A book that grew like one of these:
Nothing to hem him in or bind
But the wide limits of his mind.

Many a man who is set free
By wealth is not so wise as he.
One spends it all for his own good,
Another to bless his neighborhood,
But he was wiser, for he knew
A way to spend yet keep it too:
Made it provide him work and play,
And others, after he was clay.

I think it takes a fertile brain
To strew the golden seed like grain
Where it will grow a hundred years—
Perhaps a thousand; while it bears
Perpetual harvest through the years.
For it is clear and notable
He knew by instinct how to tell
What wealth is for. He did not tend it
Like a ewe-lamb; or hand it down
To heirs who only had to spend it;
Or try to gain a cheap renown
In monuments of bronze or stone;
Or tie it up, so it would make
A dozen lawyers fat and sleek.
He found three ways, or maybe four,
To keep it growing, till it bore
In other lives, as in his own,
Seed more golden than he had sown.

The reason, as I see it, was
He loved the permanent things, like grass
And folk and beast and wood and hill
And thinking which is never still;
So that his spirit always moves
The extended shadow of his loves.

Although he did not scorn the code
Of formal speech and civil mode,
He loved good cheer and simple ways
And honest men and the old days.
He could be stubborn and odd enough;
Like birch and maple, fibred, tough,
But like these also sweet at heart;
His humor often dry and tart
As seasoned cider, and his ire
Sudden but short, like a bush fire.
More the wise serpent than the dove,
Softening the iron with the glove,
He ruled his realm with courtly sway,
But ruled it, absolute, yea or nay.
How many stories of the guile,
How many of the canny smile
With which he always got his way!

His book, the only child he had,
Seemed to the thoughtless almost mad;
But it was only a groping, stumbling
Search of an ardent spirit, fumbling
In darkness for the truth—poetic,
But still (who knows?) perhaps prophetic.

The dreams he lived by were so clear
To him that those who lived by rule

85

Secretly thought him half a fool.
"Man who buys mountains," was their jeer.
But quietly, year after year,
He did buy mountains, one by one,
Until, the noble circle done,
Every mountain was his own—
Before, behind, right, left, the sun
Shone on his summits, his alone.

Here's something odd, yet moving too,
This buying mountains just to view;
But an apt symbol of his mind
Which always did as it inclined,
And undeterred moved to its goal:
The satisfaction of his soul.

Depend on hills, but don't rely
On men for perpetuity.
Their memory's short, and their thoughts ring
In chime with each new and untried thing.
What they remember will reveal
Not what they think but what they feel;
And this man is remembered still
Because his feelings wrote his will:
In fact, he felt so far ahead
That one can hardly call him dead.

. . . . .

I've thought, as I sat on starry nights
On Treman porch and watched the lights
Of Birch and Cherry, brighter than
The Pleiads and Aldebaran,
And heard, along the marble walk
The breeze in the sugar-maples talk

Of mountain lakes and fastnesses
And secrets more remote than these,
And smelt the wood-smoke sweet and thin
Drifting like music from the Inn—
I've thought how he would like to know
The fires are lighted, talk is free,
Books honored, science and poetry
Are living there, as long ago.

A WOMAN'S WORK

Edna Goeden

"So much to do!" She rammed dry hickory knots
Into the range, touched fire to the kindling,
Went out to fill the bucket at the pump.
Beneath her weight the handle screeched, No oil.
"If I must thaw the thing before it works
That would be nice!" she thought. But one hard thrust
Brought water, diamond in November sun.
Inside, while heat and smell of stove black spread,
She set the dishes out—blue willow ware
Her English mother brought in sixty-eight;
The plates of heavy, dull white earthenware,
Bought with the wrappers of the laundry soap.
She cut thick slabs of homemade bread, got butter,
Sliced bacon, black and odorous with smoke.
Her men came in from chores, the new milk steaming
Against their purpled hands.
                              "I'll pan the milk
Soon as the eggs are finished, Dave," she said.

He said, "No rush," but sat down at the table.
"No doughnuts?" never stirring from his place.

"Jim, get your pa some doughnuts from the crock."

The men were quiet while they stuffed the meal,
Mopping the grease and egg with buttered bread.
This morning, though, they weren't in a hurry
To get back to the barn. Dave spent too long
Stuffing his corn cob.
                              "Well?" she said at last,
Her mind on all the work she'd still to do.
"I can't tell by your smoking what you want."

Jim was the one who told:
                              "I'm getting married
Month after next. Beth promised me last night."

As if she hadn't seen this coming on!
"It took you long enough to speak your mind.
You're different from your pa."

                              Dave looked away.
"Now Liz!" he said, but sounded over pleased.
Jim laughed and put his arm around her shoulder.
"I bet it was because he had to go some
To get you from your other beaux."

                              She felt
The red come to her cheeks.
                              "Now get along.
A woman's work goes on whether or not
She's getting a new daughter."

                              Dave and Jim
Still sat and stared at her.

                              "Now what?" she asked.
"What else is there to say? Beth's a fine girl.
I can't think anyone I'd like as well."

Dave blew a puff of smoke. "What would you say
To leaving here and moving in to town?"

"Of leaving here?" Her mind could hardly take
The meaning from his words. She stacked the plates
Before she spoke: "I don't know what I'd say."

"It's like this, Liz. When Jim is married off
He'll want a farm that is his own to work.

Well, why not this one? From the rent he'd pay
Besides our savings, we could live in town.
We're not as young as we were when we married."

Her swollen knuckles told her that was so.

"And we could have a house for just us two.
It'd seem like play-work for you after this."
She watched him sharply, trying, if she could,
To catch his feeling.
                              "So it would."

                    Jim spoke:
"You've had so much to do for all these years,
Seems like you'd both deserve a spell of rest."

"So much to do!" The thought was prick enough.
"Here we go talking through a morning's work!
Tonight'll do as well for our deciding."

"Of course," Jim said.

                              The men went to the barn.
The water in the cistern of the stove
Was warm enough. She scraped and washed the dishes,
Slithering the yellow soap to make a suds.
When knives and forks were scoured so they marked
The sun upon the wall, she lugged the churn
Into the shack, began to stomp the cream.
It took a while to come. She let her eyes
Look for the threads of gray the spider looped
Across the calendar that still was June.
Churning and salting butter down was hard
In town there'd be no sense to making butter;
The general store would sell the things they'd need.
She peeled potatoes while the dusty parings

Curled in the dish. Down cellar she threw off
The heavy stone that held the mold-gray plate
And heaped a kettle with the sauerkraut.
Jim hadn't brought the eggs. The wind smelt cold
With sparkles in it, like a coming snow.
The chickens seemed to tell the weather, too—
At least their eggs were getting few enough.
If they moved off the farm, she'd not be bothered
With hens or eggs. Now there would be just time
To maybe take a lick at mending socks.
It seemed that Dave and Jim had feet enough
For centipedes, the stockings they went through.
She told them so while dishing out the dinner.
They laughed, but Dave said, "Got to keep the women
Busy at something, or the Bible says
They'll get in mischief."

                     While he winked at Jim,
She sniffed her disbelief at such remarks
Whether they were the word of God or not.
"Guess you're forgetting all the time I'd have
To squander in a town."

                     Dave looked at her:
"Decided, Liz?"

                 She shook her head. "Not yet."

When they'd gone out she started on the ironing.
White piles of coarsely woven linen grew—
The towels and scarfs, the nightgowns of the men,
Their Sunday shirts—the washed out calicoes
That she had worn through thirty married years.
"The stack don't ever seem to end," she thought.

But when the dusking came, the basket stood,
Bare to the slatted bottom, paper covered.
"And time, too, if I'm going to milk those cows,"
She said aloud and took Jim's cast off coat,
Two pails that shone like polished silver cups.
The barn was warm with breathing of the cows,
But smelled too much of horses bedded down.
She wouldn't have to come out here much longer
Unless she wished. There'd be no cows to milk,
No horse's neighing crowding through her sleep.

"We'll milk," Dave said. "You get the supper started."
She wouldn't balk at that. The night came clear,
With just above the trees a silver moon.
"It was a night like this Dave saw me home
From the church social, thirty years ago."
It seemed much longer when she felt her legs,
Clumsy from too much standing through the day.
Yet close beside her walked the girl she'd been—
Sure, even then, of what she knew was right.—
("You can't go kissing me the first time home!"—
Dave laughed: "Well, then the next!" He'd done it, too.)
There'd be more time for church and visiting
If they were off the farm. She stuffed the range
Till heat came near to crisping sliced potatoes
That fried beside the homemade sausages.
Dave looked as though his legs were hurting, too;
He walked so slow across the windy yard.
She wouldn't say a word to him tonight
If he forgot to change his overalls.
He did forget, of course, and so they could
Have eaten with the cows for all the smell.
Jim had his beauing for the Wednesday night
And made a messy splashing in the sink.

He waited till he'd dressed before he asked,
"What'll I tell Beth, Ma, about the farm?"

She was ashamed to say she didn't know.
She turned to Dave.
                    "Looks like you're letting it
Too much to me. Don't seem you want to leave."

He laid the *Farmer's Journal* on his lap
And pushed his glasses up. By that she knew
His mind was just as much in doubt as hers.
"It would be mighty fine to sleep till eight
On any day or watch the weather turn
Without a thought for crops that should be in
Or off the land."

                    She recognized those longings.
Wasn't the rooster vane above the barn
The first thing that she looked at in the morning?
And when, outside the times the children came,
Had she been still in bed at eight o'clock?
"It would be fine," she said, "except—"

                    Dave's eyes
Brightened too much at that "except." She paused.

"Except what, Liz?"

                    "What would there be to do
After we slept till eight?"

                    "You've never seen
Bill's ranch in Utah or Kate's lemon orchard
In Florida," Jim answered.

That was true.
She'd always hoped to see the children's homes.
But if it meant by giving up her own—!
Outside, the pines, their needles bright with lamplight,
Rustled a welcome to the evening wind.
She looked at Dave.

     "Don't seem as if I'd care
To leave the farm for easiness in town.
I kind of feel like one of them tall pines—
As though I'd grown too deep through all this time
To move away from here and stay alive."

Dave picked the *Journal* up again. His hands
Were trembling, but his voice was clear enough.
"You heard your ma. I guess that settles it."

Jim kissed her cheek the way he always did
Before he said goodby.

     "I guess it does."

When he'd gone out, she got her sewing basket.
Dave stared at her. "You're sure you want to stay,
Working the way you do?"

     Her nod was firm.

"I'm glad," he said, and she could hear he was.
By nine the kitchen fire lost its red,
The room turned cold against her knotted hands.
Against tomorrow's baking she set yeast
And put the bowl, well wrapt, behind the stove.
Though Dave had called "Good night" and gone to bed,
She stood, the lamplight out, beside the door.
Washed white, the yard, the barn and coop were strange.
"Like places on the moon where no one lives,"

She thought. But then the windmill clanged,
And from the barn a horse's whinny told
That life still had a thing or two to say.

"Come up to bed. There's lots to do tomorrow."

"As though I didn't know!"
                              She closed the door,
Shutting the whiteness out. Upstairs, she paused:
"No sense in getting riled at what's the truth.
I guess it wouldn't be much of a night
If there was nothing I could see I'd done
And nothing I could see I still must do."
She smiled, began undressing in the cold.

"A Woman's Work" was first published in *American Prefaces*.

ENCANTO

Jorge Guillén

La tarde que te rodea,
Bellísima, rigurosa,
Dispone a tu alrededor
Penumbra, silencio, fronda.

¡Cuánta lontananza para
Quien al amor se remonta!

Aunque en la ciudad persista
Flotando una batahola
De rumor enardecido,
El verde al silencio adora.

¡Qué apartamiento de valle,
Qué palpitación de corza!

Fatal la dicha, completa,
No puede no ser. Ahora
Todo a punto, sin alarde,
Paso a paso, ya se logra.

¡Respirar es entender,
Cuánta evidencia en la atmósfera!

Cumbre de tiempo el instante,
Se resuelve en una obra
Que ante nosotros, humildes,
Llega a perfección, se posa.

¡Junio en torno, para mí
Contigo: tú le coronas!

Déjame que espere aún,
Que mi pensamiento absorba,
Mientras a tí me abandono,
Lo profundo de tu aroma.

¡Te quiero así, desnudez,
Rendidamente remota!

96

ENCHANTMENT

Translation by Eleanor L. Turnbull

The afternoon which encircles you,
Most beautiful and austere,
Disposes around you
Faint shadow, silence, verdure.

> What a setting for
> One who aspires to love!

Although ever in the city
There is hubbub
And murmur of excited voices,
The green shades worship silence.

> What seclusion in this valley,
> What trembling of fallow deer!

Complete happiness is inevitable,
It cannot but be. Now
All is prepared, without show,
Step by step, it comes.

> To breathe is to understand,
> What evidence in the atmosphere!

Acme of time, the instant
Melts into achievement
Which before us, humble ones,
Arrives at perfection, alights.

> June is everywhere for me
> With you, you crown it!

Permit me still to wait
Till my thought absorbs
The depths of your fragrance,
While I give myself up to you.

> I love you thus, unadorned,
> Submissively remote!

Déjame que todavía
Te sueñe como una ópera
Que de pronto se encendiera
Para mí, deslumbradora,
Mágica ante mi embelso,
Y aunque tan real, tan próxima,
Entre sus luces se alzara
Siempre inaccesible: diosa.
(Tu más divina hermosura
Canta en secreto victoria.)

Middlebury, Noviembre de 1938

Permit me still to dream of you
As a dazzling opera
That suddenly may kindle magic for me
To my ravishment,
And though so real and so near,
Between its lights may arise,
Forever inaccessible:
A goddess.
Whose heavenly beauty
In secret sings victory.

Note: A metrical form has not been attempted in this translation, as the poet
preferred a more literal rendering—E. L. T.   42675

Ripton Gorge

LUNAR MOTH

Robert Hillyer

From the forest of night
Comes the magic, the light
Green-wingèd flight—
Titania come
To a mortal's home
From the low-moon land
With her wings and her wand
And her bright black eyes
And her tiny feet
And her wings pale green
Like wind through wheat.
Now I am wise,
For now I have seen
Men told no lies
Of a fairy queen.
She was here on the wall,
And now she has gone,
Quiet, small,
To the night, alone.
With a wave of her wand
She vanished, beyond
The sky to the cool
Moon of July.

SHE SHOULD HAVE LIVED IN OTHER DAYS

Doris McLaury Hughson

She should have lived in other days,
When windows arched to Heaven,
And every yeoman and his dame
Could count all sins in seven.

She should have met the Wife of Bath
Beside some far church door,
And heard how Jankin came to wear
The shoes of Number Four.

The leper at her gate had fared
As well as England's king;
Stories of Boulogne and Ypres
Would have spiced his victualing.

Each palmer would have gone his way,
Full belly and whole cloak,
And Christmas found the parson with
A fat pig in his poke.

Sweeter far than galingale
To sauce a swan at night
Had been the tales she told of wakes,
By fire and candlelight.

She should have lived in other days.
She drives a lusty Ford;
The travelling salesmen come to her
To get their room and board.

She knows the way to each man's heart,
And counts three wedding rings;
Girls go to her for sound advice
About their lovemakings.

She sells pieced quilts in a church booth
At Sawgus County Fair,
And lays a bet of fifty cents
On old Zeb Perkins' mare.

She finds the way to Heaven good
And takes things as they are,
With time for loves and voyaging,
And Crumbtown's Church Bazaar.

"She Should Have Lived in Other Days" first appeared in the New York *Herald Tribune*.

HOSPITAL NOCTURNE

Christie Jeffries

The corridor is a white blaze
Burning against the shadowy grays
Of half-shut doors. A monotone
Of silence punctuates the drone
Of footfalls, interrupts the rush
To where the wings of blackness brush
Wan faces or importunate
Life clamors at the threshold gate.

Within the many-bedded ward
Pain rules, defiant overlord
Of sleep. Long pencilled lines of light
Merge in the ebony of night,
Reminders of the eyes awake
To tragedy and dull heartbreak,
Of lips that soothe and hands that bless,
Prodigal of tenderness.

"Hospital Nocturne" first appeared in *Spirit*.

SKY BETWEEN BUILDINGS

Burges Johnson

As I go prosing on my way,
  Quite busily amid the throng,
The common sounds of every day
  Engage me while I trudge along.
Till all at once some part of me,
Some secret inner heart of me,
  Will catch the echo of a song.
It is not formed from any tone
  The city's myriad lips create,
Nor yet the voice of steel and stone
  Grown suddenly articulate.
Some other world that dwells apart
  I know is breathless in its thrall,—
While down into my pulsing heart
  These few arresting measures fall.
One fleeting dream is built of it—
The sweet elusive lilt of it—
  Then as a dream I lose it all.

I think that somewhere, far or near,
  Lurk all the songs as yet unsung;
And music we have yet to hear
  From ghostly strings is there outflung.
It cannot be so far, I know,
  Beyond the reaching souls of men,
For there are favored ones who go
  And dwell there and return again.
But I—I do not know the way!
  So, prosily amid the throng
I heed the sounds of every day,—
  The city's voices, hoarse and strong,

Till suddenly some part of me,
Some secret inner heart of me,
    Hears just the echo of a song.
One fleeting dream is built of it,
And then the very lilt of it
    Has vanished as I trudge along.

CITY ANTS

Burges Johnson

Some hulking giant with a rake of steel
Into my mete of earth has marked a hundred ruts,
Parallel and strait and close together;
And then has raked again from side to side,
Until the harried earth is criss-crossed deep.
I cannot see him at his work he bulks so large;
I only know he hides the sun. I only hear
And feel the jarring rhythm of his toil;
And smell his reek, and dread
The swift oblivion of his heavy heel.
I know some world-old purpose drives him on
To wield his tools, and blight spontaneous things,
And plant his seeds of iron.
                                             But I trudge
In paths I have not chosen, moiling on
With other ants, by geometric ways,
Just back and forth and back and forth
Through narrow canyons that lead nowhere else
Save into others grimmer, more uncompromising.
Somewhere I know there must be roods of ground
Not bound and harried, where I might
Try winding paths, or break a bit of trail,
And build my little hill, and see the distances.
And yet—I might be lonely. Here there are
Five million other pismires like myself.

OLD KETHMANN

Herbert Krause

Pockerbrush folk were used to Kethmann's lights
Winking with yellow eyes at ten o'clock—
"Aint played out yet, be you?"
The neighbors shut and hooked their gates and smiled:
"The old man's at it kinda late agin,"
And went inside to ease off heavy shoes.

Across his farm he plodded back and forth,
Never the first one done with season's work,
Nor yet the last: just middling fair along.
He hung his farm about his neck, they said,
And let it drag him shoulder-round and bent.

Before a rooster flapped at dawn
His hazy coal-oil beam jerked on from barn
To shed and back; and midnight stirred and breathed,
Crowding against his lantern's sleepy ray.

For most of us the waking hour of five
Was hardly stranger six days of the week.
But Sundays Kethmann kindled up his wick
Earlier.—The neighbors whetted eyes
And meeting at the blacksmith shop or store,
Chewed over news. "I can't think when he sleeps,
If sleep he does."
            "I kinda guess the why
Of it and all, being it's his, is his."

But once the blacksmith with a twinkle said,
"How is it you've a light early Sundays
When most of us turn over forty winks?"
Old Kethmann took them in a single look,
The half a dozen gathered at the shop
With broken odds to mend and thoughts to air,
While raindrops "turned about" to drum the roof.
His silence held them in a pocket grip.
He counted out his silver for the job
With care, dime by dime aloud, a quarter
Piece looked over twice, into a leathered hand.
Their time was his, to him. At last he said,
"Starting off ahead an hour or so,
Like that, figure to get a long day's rest."

BEGGAR'S SNOW

Herbert Krause

The cold and trickling rain
And a yellow leaf
Lifting an edge
Against the brittle clash
Of sleet on tin and lash
Of wind along the street:
So much I saw
Before he stumbled by,
A rag-end of the river lanes—
Or what was left of him
In gray November weather.

He buried what he could of chin and fingers
Under cloth of one thin coat;
Bent like grass
In storm. Harried
By the white cord-ends of snow,
He shuffled off and lost
Identity among the flakes...slow...slow...

RISK

Marion LeMoyne Leeper

Who defeats great grief must be
A master of rare surgery.

A hair-keen scalpel he must take
And cut the heart from its deep ache;

This is a daring thing to do
For though the blade slips neatly through—

Sometimes incisions fester where
None but a wizard's knife would dare,

For nothing but a labored breath
Then separates the heart from death—

From death, still quick, but as profound
As if a man lay underground.

JOHN MacELMAIN

Louise McNeill

He was the strongest man on Gauley fork,
Could jump a six rail fence without a start,
Hold two full wheat sacks straight above his head,
And tear a knot of hickory clean apart.

One day while clearing off some ground for corn
A wind-bent tree fell up, not down, the hill
And caught him as he ran. From that day on
The muscles in his legs were flat and still.

For twenty years he kept his rocking chair,
The dictionary open on his knees.
It was his only book. He learned it all
From A a r to Xs, Ys, and Zs.

He had the definitions and could spell
Phthisic and asafetida and gnu,
And many harder ones, ungodly words,
The folks must not suspicion that he knew.

He liked to stump the school marm and the priest,
To see The Colonel's jaw thrust out and fall,
And by that holy book he swore young John
Should rub his back against a college wall.

GRANNY SAUNDERS

Louise McNeill

Her ministration was to heal
With pungent herb and bitter peel.
Up in the drying loft she hung
Horehound and sage and blacksnake-tongue,
Wild cherry, spice bush, penny "rorrel,"
Blue monkshood, ginseng, sour sorrel,
Thin twisted stalks, sharp jimpson weeds,
Bloody percoons, hot mustard seeds,
And meadow docks—both broad and narrow,
Rough bone-set, golden thread and yarrow,
Field balsam, catnip, dittany,
All to be simmered down to tea.

All to be brewed for aches and ills—
Red pepper pods for croup and chills;
Spearmint for phthisic; flax for pain;
Horseradish roots for bruise or sprain;
And for uncertain maladies
The northwest bark of dogwood trees.

"Granny Saunders" first appeared in *American Prefaces*.

NORA KANE

Louise McNeill

She was a Kane and the Kanes were white trash
Who lived in a cabin up Peasant run.
They seasoned their fodder beans with groundhog,
Borrowed their grub stuff and stole for fun.

All of the Kanes had the Old Nick's temper.
Their feet sashayed to a fiddle's tune,
And they could go to a patch of ginseng
Like their hound dogs followed a corn fed coon.

Zeb Sage was old when he married Nora
To brute and carry and do his will,
And the Sages called her a scheming hussy,
But she ruled the Sages and rules them still.

Her brown feet jigged to the hymns they quavered,
Her hot blood swept through their frigid veins,
She signed her X in their family Bible
And filled their cradles with swarthy Kanes.

"Nora Kane" first appeared in *Poetry*.

MOUNTAINS AND A MAN

A Glimpse of Joseph Battell

Charles Malam

i.

Tell you a tale of mountains and of men?
Tell rather of a man who was a mountain.
Up where they name their mountains after men,
Or short of big men, after what men live by—
I'm thinking now of Lincoln and of Bread Loaf—
His name is written for the world in granite,
His name is written for a cornerstone,
An anchor stone to hold a bridge of granite.
Any tourist, asking for the Inn,
May read in passing, never losing mileage.
"Joseph Battell." The spelling must be right,
He put it there himself, the scoffers say.
He was a cornerstone. He was a bridge.
He had a right to put it there himself.

ii.

Vermont in spring, where spring from trying buds
And leaf designs and color schemes in branches
In cities south along the sanddrift coasts
Comes suddenly at dawn some late May morning,
Languid and warm, smelling of wet earth turning—
Vermont in spring, and spring in Middlebury,
And Joe Battell came up the road from Cornwall.
A farmer crossed a yard, carrying milk.
The dark wood buckets rubbed his muddied boots.
"Good morning, Mister."
                    "Morning."
                              "Thawing weather.

The ground back there feels ready for the plow.
This sun will pull the frost out by the roots."
"I reckon so."
                        "Mind if I have a drink?"
"Come in. Jest help yourself."
                        The road was soft,
Or what would be a road another month,
But what was yard was softer. What was mud?
"Here, here's a dipper jest inside the door here.
Better take milk. I ain't cleared out the spring yet."
The milk was warm. It foamed against the metal.
"You're Phil Battell's boy, ain't ye?"
                        "Yes, I'm Joseph."
"Out pretty early, if it's mud you're after.
It takes a morning sun to grow real mud."
They smiled their mutual knowledge of Dame Nature.
"I thought I'd have a walk before first class."
"Nothing like air to help your Latin settle.
Looks kind of pretty, down the valley there.
Somebody's wakeful in the dormitory—
You're going to college, ain't ye?"
                        "I'm in college."
He coughed and held a mitten to his mouth.
"That's Starr Hall, with the smoke above the chimney."
"Bad cough you've got there. Fill the dipper up.
It's half an hour to breakfast yet, and home."
"The cough's inside. I talked with Mr. Brainerd;
He says the hill air ought to do it good.
He spoke to me of Ripton. That's good milk."
The farmer grunted. "Raised the cows myself.
I was in lumbering, up Thetford way.
The trees got spindly, and the camp broke up,
And so I turned to cows."
                        A thread of smoke

116

Drifted above the pines a mile beyond.
From where they stood, they almost looked down hill.
"Fine view here."
            "So it is."
                        "Well, thank you."
                                "Sure.
Come back sometime and have another dipper.
If you go up to Ripton, see Arn Atwood."
"I shall. I've heard of him from Mr. Brainerd."

One mile of wagon ruts and slippery clay.
Down hill, then up hill, then another down hill.
This was a country mostly of horizons.
Young Joe Battell leaned on the snakerail fence.
Perhaps it would be Ripton, after all.
A farmhouse, with the cows to milk at four,
Warm milk, the pungent sting of cow-sheds, forage,
The sour-sweet corn in silo, sunrise making
Thin lanes of dust and cobweb through the stanchions.
Maybe a horse worth driving on a half-day.
Fine view here from the hill. If I were building,
Where could I better build of far horizons?
Or any man, if he were building dreams?
A man could build a world of these hills only!

He coughed and started down the road to town.

                        iii.

Vermont in August, and a flag of dust
Drifting among the trees far down the valley
To mark the way the road unwinds itself
Before it shakes off elm trees, maple trees,
Chokecherry brush and fern and elderbush
To straighten sharply, cushioned deep in sand,

By lawn and sleepy orchard and piazza—
Vermont in August, and the fields in hay,
And Joe Battell came up the road from Ripton.

He drove black Morgans, dancing in the shafts.
Their dainty feet mocked at the wheels pursuing.
He brought three ladies, young and quick and laughing,
Their flowers and bonnets and their nets and flounces
Dancing against the breeze the Morgans made.

"Boyce! Where's Tom Boyce! Somebody find me Boyce!"
He swung himself to ground. "Here, help the ladies.
Somebody find me Boyce! Now, beauties, now!"
Keeping the reins in one hand, firm. "You, Sammy,
Go find me—There you are! Tom, hitch the buggy.
Some fool has started cutting timber out
This side the gorge. Go stop it! Here now, ladies,
Your hands, please. This is Bread Loaf.—Tom, in Ripton
See if the mail is in. We passed the stage
Just as we started climbing.—Now, then, ladies,
What do you think of it, eh? What d'ya say?
Bread Loaf!—Don't be afraid, the team is gentled.
Here, let me show you. Sammy, take the reins."
A big arm up, and while their nets still fluttered
The three young women barely touching foot
Were out of carriage and upon the turf.

"Take a good look. You'll never take enough.
I tell all, help yourself to mountain ranges!
There's always still another for the taking!
Where's Mrs. Robinson? Three more for supper,
And extra helpings of the frozen stuff.
I'm warm as sunset over Hurricane.
Here, Sammy, take the team to stable. Supper!
The girl will show you ladies to your rooms!"

Vermont, and summer, and the sun gone down
Like thin green gold beyond the western range,
And twilight folding softly down from Bread Loaf.
The porch that faced the west was deep in shadows.
Joseph Battell was talking with the shadows.

There is New York. That is the world's, and welcome.
But all the rest you see—there, over there,
And there—all mine. The mountains, and the forests,
All mine, the smallest fern curled in the dew.
I climbed the road there thirty years ago.
It wasn't like this, thirty years ago.
The trees were wood, the mountains, any man's.
It wasn't very large, the world I had.
It didn't ask for size, to last as long
As I might last, I thought then. Thirty years.
There was a farmhouse, and an apple orchard,
The fields, and nothing else, nothing but mountains.
Mountains beneath the trees, beyond the trees,
And rocky in the east, old Bread Loaf Mountain.
I thought they must be watching me, those mountains,
Asking who was I standing on the porch there,
Standing in the twilight, my own twilight.
I was my father's son, but who was that?
Was I a friend? What had I put a name to?
There was a voice of axes in the mountains,
The snarl of sawmills when the axes rested.
Who are you, asked the mountains, and I answered
One not long with you, and they answered back
As long perhaps as we shall be with you.
They're killing us, the axes and the saws.
A man with steel enough can kill a mountain.
A man can tear it down to boulder bone,
Strip flesh of foliage and nerve of roots out,

Lay it bare open to the rain and thunder,
Lay it defenseless to the quiet frost.
A man can bring a mountain down to dust,
And after, find he brought himself to dust,
Himself and children and his children's children.
Who are you, asked the mountains, looking at me.
I was afraid. What could I tell them, watching?
Joseph Battell! Could I shout that at mountains?
Joseph Battell! And briefly come to visit:
I haven't long to stay. Could I shout that?

I walked old lumber roads. I followed deer tracks.
I watched the cattle, where they climbed to clearings
No man that other man remembered, made.
I climbed to clearings, too, and there were others.
The mountains could be quiet, free of axes.
There was no need of steel shouting and snarling
Among the birches and the higher pine.
Let the steel learn its place, and keep its place.
This was a world was built for trees, for peace.
This was a world, I said, should keep its peace.
Let me but keep the world a little while
And I would see what one small man could do
To hold the trees for mountains, and for peace.

The mountains let me stay. The mountains saved me.
Now I have saved the mountains.
                            "Hello, Tom.
Come on, draw up a chair. I'm only thinking.
You find that fellow who was cutting timber?
I thought so. Did you get his name to paper?
Good man. He doesn't know it, counting dollars,
But some day he'll sleep sounder in his grave,
Having no maple murders on his mind.

They say I'm crazy, don't they, Tom? Well, John does.
John's blunter'n you. That's all right. I am crazy.
Some one has got to be these times, I guess,
If only to hold sane ones down to earth
By being example of what not to be.

"Isn't it fine, Tom, down there, down the valley?
Gives us some room to grow in, don't it, Tom?"

iv.

Keep north from Rutland. All hard surface roads.
You'll come to Salisbury Plains, or if you're lucky
And lose yourself, you'll come by Dunmore Lake.
Keep north, and then you'll come to Middlebury.
His name is written there in brick and granite,
A cornerstone, an archstone for a bridge,
Something to put a hand to and to swear to,
Something to read and never stop your engine.
But if you stop, or for some cause stay over,
And walking, find the bridge, and there cross over,
You'll find his name written in more than granite.
You'll find his name written in men and women
Who never knew him and may never know him
But who grow bigger in the space he left them.
"Joseph Battell." He's writing it himself.
It takes a lifetime, telling how to say it.

SUNSET AT BREAD LOAF

Charles Malam

When meadow larks are dust and delicate bones,
When the thrush of summer sings no more on the hill
And they come with spades to turn the river stones
Seeking the visible voice forever still,
When the man and his horse and the plow that turned the clover
And the skull of the bee are legends to bracket together
And iron works the peculiar fossils over
In that other world, in that unfamiliar weather,

Will they know what they have not found, those other folk,
Where they stand thigh deep in the red and lavender grass
Under the smoke-ringed sun? Will they stoop and stroke
The fragile carbonates, knowing they, too, must pass
To a thought, to a dream, to a song, its lost words ended,
Sad as this day was sad, and wholly splendid?

ONE HOUR FROM DAWN

Charles Malam

One hour from dawn, and cold and chill,
Coming down from the dripping wood
I met a red fox in the clearing.
On three startled legs he stood,

Lean and weary and showing age.
Perhaps the scent of man was lost
In damp blueberry and pasture sage;
Perhaps the cold hill brook I crossed

Washed me scentless of all but name
And little of that to caution fear.
He saw me come from the edge of light;
On three stiff legs he watched me near.

Where silence leaps with teeth of steel,
Where darkness bites through fur and bone
In the first dew, in the early morning,
Who but the hunter walks alone?

Unguarded in the waking light
Two shadows in the dew-bent grass
Waited to see what the other hunted.
    He was the first to nod and pass.

Gilmore Cottage, Bread Loaf, 1930

"One Hour from Dawn" was chosen for an award of $25.00, among the short lyrics
submitted for *The Bread Loaf Anthology.*

REASSURANCE

Jeannette Martin

If you would discover the reason why
A man will hollow the haunch of a hill
To build a hurricane cellar, though
He and his children all will die
And leave unopened the heavy door—
If you are a stranger and would know,
Ask a man living where life has been
Familiar with death too often for
One to be unaware of all
The meaning coiled in a lash of wind
Or stutter of rain upon the sill—
He can explain the reason for
A years-unopened hurricane door.
The heart has need of a cellar like this,
A hill to back believing against
When wind uncoils its hissing intent
And storm betrays what the warning meant.

BELIEF

Jeannette Martin

Mountain or sky...Who can say
Where one begins and the other ends?
Hope for any reply depends
On the shadowy whim
Of this early fog,
Noncommittal as dawn itself
Caught between dark and a doubtful day.

Who can say...Mountain or sky?
Nothing is definite, nothing known,
No horizon where birds have flown.
But we who have waited
For wings at dawn
Know we can trust an early fog
And believe in an ultimate reply.

MALISON

Enid Morgan

The ale-wife laughs by the tavern door
The hangman sleeps in his bed,
But pishogue will grow on the bone-white floor
And the witching fires burn red.

Though church bells toll through the frosty air
And yeomen tell their beads,
The good wheat chokes in the thriving tare
And a black hawk picks the seeds.

May heath berry cover the rusted plow,
The dun mare die in foal
Since my love hangs from a greenwood bough
And a hedge priest shrives his soul.

ON A CHILD KILLED IN A SPANISH AIR-RAID

Theodore Morrison

This refuse was a city yesterday
Until the bombers came, sheared roofs from walls,
Bared rooms, trepanned dark stairways, wormy halls;
Thus Nero ripped his mother's womb, they say.
The steel hawks, mousing for their deafened prey,
Splintered this tenement. Death plunged right through,
Tossed out men's privacies, and pitched down too
A child among the powdered lime and clay.

Ah, what a hate must prompt so foul a shame!
But child, they are not so human as to hate,
The keen technicians and the lords of state
Who dropped the exploding death. Their present aim
Is trial merely; they observe and wait,
Honing their edges for a vaster game.

IN THE BATTELL HEMLOCKS

Fred Lewis Pattee

Deep in the Northern Lands
Where mountains are, and man may be alone,
Where nothing breaks the silence save the moan
Of slumbering forests and the eagle's cry
Above the peaks that lone and nameless lie,
Vast, shaggy, wild, unscathed by human hands
A hemlock forest stands.

So black it is and drear,
'Tis dark at mid-day, and at night there shines no star;
And save the owl's, heard weirdly from afar,
Within its deeps no voice of beast or bird,
And on its velvet floors no sound is heard
Save when at fearsome noon the timorous deer
May seek a refuge here.

Long may the deadly fire
And deadlier axe be far, for in my soul
I love the hemlock with his shaggy bole,
His wild grotesquery, and his daintiness
In days of June, his glorious summer dress,
His head among the clouds, his call..."Aspire!
The hills are high—be higher!''

I too would fly to thee,
O sheltering hemlock, brother of my soul,
Beneath thy dome I hear the organ roll
Of worlds unknown. I too would fight
Like thee the blast, the coming winter night,
With thee my soul awakes and I am free!
Hail, brother hemlock tree!

THE WIDOW'S CLEARING

Samuel B. Pettengill

Beauty was there,
And peace,
And the strength of the hills.
So they came.
They came a long ways,—
Came from across the Atlantic,
Up the Connecticut,
Up the White River,
Across the Divide,—
Up to the clearing.
It took a long time—
Four generations.

The view was wonderful.
The grass tasted good to the oxen;
There were trout in the stream;
And deer on the mountain,
And the sugar maples were sweet in the spring.

They stayed a long time—
Four generations—
From Bunker Hill to the Klondyke.
The axe and the scythe,
The plow and the cradle
Did their work.
Finally the tide moved on,—
On to Michigan, Iowa, Oregon.
The boys went West,
And the girls married boys
Who went West.

There was work out there,
Out there in the West.
So they took the axe and the scythe,
The plow and the cradle.
Only the widow stayed.
Finally she went—
West.

Scrub apples and thistles
And immortelles.
The clearing is smaller now,
Smaller.
The pines and the spruce and the hemlocks
Have resumed their march.

Only the hills are there,
And beauty,
And peace.

"The Widow's Clearing" first appeared in the Middlebury *News Letter*.

FORTY TO TWENTY

Hazel B. Poole

Put off your hard bright armor if you will.
You are safe; we shall not hurt you any more.
Nor can you wound us now; your trumpets shrill
Against the deafness of a closing door.

The field is yours; the citadel is ours.
You have no fortress like the final grace
Of those who in the shelter of doomed towers
Wear, in the twilight of a changing face,
The sudden beauty of late asters white
In the dusk of woods; out of a fall of lace
Their shoulders curving smooth in candle-light;
Their heads, still dark, turned with a moment's trace
Of swift, bright youth, faint as an echoing horn
Across the hills; the loveliness of years
Now gathered close, a shadowy garment worn
As their sole armor in a place of fears.

Turn from our gate; you do not vex our thought.
Against another foeman's conquering word
Out of this last frail beauty we have wrought
In our last fires a brief and terrible sword.

Split Rails

TO THOSE UNSUSPECTING

Madeline Reeder

Let the red fox dig his pointed nose
In ferns by moonlight,
The sky hollow where the moon just rose
With all fields turned white.

Let the lynx crouch low to autumn
Under black hemlock . . .
Obsequies to this season done
In the light stalk

Of animal foot and the hushed, hot breath
Of their furred bodies:
Let them gesture, the doomed-to-their-death,
The foxes, the trees,

Under the moonlight before we grieve;
Let these seasonal few—
We die every autumn before we leave—
Take their adieu

Unsuspecting, unwarned, unheeded
In an attitude
Of customary living seeded
With death let them take their last breath.

CAUCE Y VUELO
Pedro Salinas

Entre el trino del pájaro
y el son grave del agua.
El trino se tenía
en la frágil garganta;
la garganta en un bulto
de plumas, en la rama;
y la rama en el aire;
y el aire, en cielo, en nada.
El agua iba rompiéndose
entre piedras. Quebrado
su fluir misterioso
en los guijos, clavada
en su lecho, apoyada
en la tierra, tocándola
lloraba
de tener que tocarla.
Tú vacilaste: era
la luz de la mañana.
Y yo, entre los dos cantos,
tu elección aguardaba.
¿Qué irías a escoger,
entre el trino del pájaro,
fugitivo capricho,
—escaparse, volarse—,
o los destinos fieles,
hacia su mar, del agua?

"Cauce y Vuelo" first appeared in *Razón de Amor*.

EARTH OR AIR

Translation by Eleanor L. Turnbull

Trilling of bird song
and grave sound of water.
The trill
in a fragile throat;
the throat in a tuft
of feathers on a bough;
the bough in the air;
and the air, in sky, in nothing.
The water shattered
between stones, its mysterious
flowing broken by pebbles,
fixed in its channel, resting
on earth, touching it,
and weeping
for having to touch it.
You hesitating
in the light of morning.
And I, between the two songs,
awaiting your choice.
Which will you choose,
the trilling of the bird,
fleeting fancy,
—to escape, to fly—
or, following its true destiny
to the sea, the water?

LA FALSA COMPAÑERA

Pedro Salinas

Yo estaba descansando
de grandes soledades
en una tarde dulce
que parecía casi
tan tierna como un pecho.
Sobre mí, ¡qué cariño
vertían, entendiéndolo
todo, las mansas sombras,
los rebrillos del agua,
los trinos, en lo alto!
¡Y de pronto la tarde
se acordó de sí misma
y me quitó su amparo!
¡Qué vuelta dió hacia ella!
¡Qué extática, mirándose
en su propia belleza,
se desprendió de aquel
pobre contacto humano,
que era yo, y me dejó,
también ella, olvidado!
El cielo se marchó
gozoso, a grandes saltos
—azules, grises, rosas,—
a alguna misteriosa
cita con otro cielo
en la que le esperaba
algo más que la pena
de estos ojos de hombre
que le estaban mirando.
Se escapó tan deprisa
que un momento después

THE FAITHLESS FRIEND

Translation by Eleanor L. Turnbull

After great loneliness
and longing
I was resting
on an evening almost as
tender as a woman's breast.
Soothing shadows of trees,
reflections on the water,
and warbling in the heavens,
were shedding over me
an all-comprehending love.
And then, all at once,
the evening came to herself
and robbed me of her shelter.
What a return to herself!
How full of ecstasy,
gazing at her own beauty,
did she rid herself
of that poor human contact
which was I! She too left me
alone, forgotten.
The sky departed joyful,
with great leaps and bounds,
—blue, grey and rose—
to some mysterious meeting
with another sky,
where there was waiting
something more than the suffering
of those grieving eyes of man
with their sorrowful gaze.
So swift the flight of the sky
that but a moment after

ya ni siquiera pude
tocarlo con la mano.
Los árboles llamaron
su alegría hacia adentro;
no pude confundir
a sus ramas con brazos
que a mi dolor se abrían.
Toda su vida fué
a hundirse en las raíces:
egoísmo del árbol.
La lámina del lago
negándome mi estampa,
me dejó abandonado
a este cuerpo hipotético;
sin la gran fe de vida
que da el agua serena
al que no está seguro
de si vive, y la mira.
Todo se fué. Los píos
más claros de los pájaros
ya no los comprendía.
Inteligibles eran
para otras aves; ya
sin cifra para el alma.
Yo estaba solo, solo.
Solo con mi silencio;
solo, si lo rompía,
también, con mis palabras.
Todo era ajeno, todo
se marchaba a un quehacer
incógnito y remoto,
en la tierra profunda,
en los cielos lejanos.
Implacable, la tarde

I could not even touch it
with my eager outstretched hand.
The trees summoned their rapture
back into their hearts.
I could no longer
mistake their branches for arms
reaching out to my sorrow.
All of their life sank once more
deep, deep into their roots:
the selfishness of trees!
The smooth surface of the lake,
disowning my impression,
now left me given over
to this supposèd body,
without the great faith in life
which untroubled water gives
to one who is not sure
if he lives and gazes on it.
All were departed. I could
understand no longer
the clearest piping of birds,
now intelligible only
to other birds, and without
a cipher known to my soul.
I was alone, so alone.
Alone with my silence,
and alone also even
if I broke it with my speech.
All was alien to me, all
moved towards affairs
unknown, remote,
in the depths of the earth,
in the far-away heavens.
The evening, relentless,

me estaba devolviendo
lo que fingió quitarme
antes: mi soledad.
Y entre reflejos, vientos,
cánticos y arreboles,
se marchó hacia sus fiestas
trascelestes, divinas,
salvada ya de aquella
tentación de un instante
de compartir la pena
que un mortal la llevaba.
Aun volvió la cabeza;
y me dijo, al marcharse,
que yo era sólo un hombre,
que buscara a los míos.
Y empecé, cuesta arriba,
despacio, mi retorno
al triste techo oscuro
de mí mismo: a mi alma.
El aire parecía
un inmenso abandono.

was restoring to me
what she feigned to rob me of
before: my solitude.
And amid reflections, wind,
twilight song, sunset colors,
she moved towards her festival,
heavenly, divine,
saved now from that
temptation of a moment
to share in the sorrow
a mortal had brought her.
But nevertheless she turned
and spoke to me as she went,
telling me I was but man,
bidding me seek my own kind.
Thus I began the uphill
slow climb of my return
to the sad gloomy roof
of myself: to my soul.
The air seemed now to be nought
but an immense desertion.

FOR A FAUN IN CAPTIVITY

Leota E. Schoff

O Mother of all wild and helpless things,
A few short weeks and you must take your child
Back to his forest home; to you he brings
His faunhood's innocence not yet beguiled,
A trusting heart, soft eyes that must acquire
The look of fear. Too soon the graceful leap
He makes to lick my fingers through the wire
Will take the backwood's fence and brushwood heap.
Against that day when hunters come, prepare
Beneath the fallen oak the deepest bed,
The darkest forest path, the secret lair,
The tallest ferns to hide that lifted head.
And teach him, Nature, gently as you can,
That he has never known the ways of man!

IMPROMPTU

(Written for a friend at Star Island)

Dallas Lore Sharp

Here is no tree, no burning bush
    Where God and I may meet,
But Star and White and Appledore
    Were planted for God's feet.

And though the sea swings far around,
    And overhead the sky,
Yet Appledore and White and Star
    Are in God's loving eye.

And when the fog wraps Appledore,
    And night falls over Star,
The light on White the fisher tells
    Where God and Harbor are.

"Impromptu" first appeared in the *Christian Register*.

WHILE BOBOLINK WAS HERE

Dallas Lore Sharp

I heard him when the reeds were young
    Along a clover sea;
Above the heading waves he hung,
And o'er the purple waters flung
    His storm of ecstasy.

It swifter swept than gray mist floats,
    It broke like shining spray;
The tempest of his tossing notes
Were poured as from a thousand throats
    Across the fragrant bay.

His dress was gay as this gay song;
    He woke before the light;
His only task the glad day long
Was singing, swinging, there among
    The meadow flowers bright.

But now the tall reeds, withered, wave
    About a meadow gray,
And Bobolink is dumb and grave,
He's lost the song and suit so brave
    He had when it was May.

The dreamy day and frosty night
    I hear his peevish cry;
He's swift upon his southern flight
To meads that never black with blight,
    Nor white with winter lie.

He's left the meadow, burnt and hot,
  He's left me lone and drear;
But still within the white-birch lot
Cheeps Chickadee—whom I forgot
  While Bobolink was here!

"While Bobolink Was Here" first appeared in *Zion's Herald*.

PINES OF GOOD WILL

Dallas Lore Sharp

The winds, aloft in the moving trees,
Surf-sounds of softly breaking seas,
Over a shifting shoal of leaves,
  Along the shores of pine.

Sweetly and low the night winds play
Their lullabies at close of day,
'Mong—gently, nature's cradles they,
  The dark pine trees.

Here deepest shades brood over all,
Mingled and mixed, where moon-beams fall,
In sifted streams through pine tops tall,
  In sleepy sympathy.

And all is dark with shadows sweet,
The brown leaves laid beneath our feet
Wake not, but sleep unending sleep
  In fragrant gloom.

The green leaves nod, and dreaming, sigh;
The night winds float in slumber by,
Murmuring songs from a distant sky,
  To the listening pines.

And undisturbed by our silent tread,
A bird sleeps sheltered overhead,
Secure in its lofty, wind-swayed bed,
  And dreams.

His head tucked 'neath his weary wing,
He's lulled as the night winds softly sing,
He sleeps as the pine trees gently swing,
  In his cradle high.

Dreamily murmur the drowsy winds,
Sleepily sway the shadowy pines,
Safely, sweetly the still night finds,
    Her tired children sleeping.

And nestling all beneath her wing,
Night winds and stars together sing,
Pine trees and worlds together swing
    And sleep and sleep.

"Pines of Good Will" first appeared in *Good Will Record*.

NARRATIVE OF SNOW

Israel Smith

With no more warning than the fugitive
Impulse of movement gulls might give,

Between me and the winter sun's obscure
Declension, snow whirled to immure

My body in a swift oblivion
No ruse of running could outrun,

To sting my face with icy ache,
A savage sky dissolving, flake by flake,

In stars of fury, intricate and chill,
Aligned to taunt all artifice of will.

One small, anonymous, dazed man,
Trapped without subterfuge or plan,

I braced my individual pride
To turn catastrophe aside,

But stood involved within a universe
Of frosty malice blowing like a curse.

I stood and watched the shape of speed reveal
Imperial disaster at his heel,

And saw the waving ground become
Merged with the insane air's delirium.

Caught in obliteration's cold circumference,
Sheer rage of snow confuting quick defense,

No farmer's lantern swinging back the dark,
No hailing voice to make my voice less stark,

I stood against the force of snow, snow-drowned,
My single strategy my own heart's sound.

ONLY ON THE WEST WIND

Florida Watts Smyth

ONLY ON THE WEST WIND

Only on the west wind comes the whistle of trains
Down in the valley. Only then we hear
The world go past, crowded in every car.
Reading the latest news, the travelers sit
Turning and folding. Little we know of it.
When was it the train stopped down there and we,
As unrelated as a ship at sea
To the last rumors of war and violence,
Became involved in magical events
Ignored by printers: oracles in trees,
Loud winds that speak and mountain mysteries?
Only on the west wind comes the whistle of trains.

HAY WAGON

There's hay on every bush. That's how I know
It's down this lane the broad hay wagons go.
I see the first one swaying through the trees
And draw back in the fern up to my knees.
The heavy team holds back; the man on top
Stoops to avoid a limb, pulls down his cap
As the leaves brush by. Zigzagging down the lane
The roving collie catches up again.

I Walked With A Bird Once

I walked with a bird once, just for a dozen
Runs, with pauses between. You'll guess
That this was a robin. They have that odd habit
    Of movement and watchfulness

Birds are all nerve and wing; hasty, shy.
    When I fall in step,
    They take to wings and fly.

Widow's Clearing

They call this Widow's Clearing and you see
    That pile o' stone?
That's where the house stood that the widow lived in
    For years, alone.

Nobody seems to know why her husband left her;
    Just started out
One day to go for the mail down there in the valley.
    What the trouble was about,

If there was any trouble, nobody seemed to know.
    He wasn't in the brook;
There was no use looking for him; there wasn't any
    Place to look.

Sometimes I used to see her driving the cow home,
    Summer nights.
She was a quiet woman, never complaining;
    But stood by her rights.

She had a gun. No, she wasn't that kind.
    It was nothing you could get at.
We figgered he just got tired doing the chores.
    She did 'em after that.

HAZARD

I

This barn by the road will fall down soon.
How soon would you say?
They have shored it up at this end with a brace
And stabled the horse. He's skin and bone.
If I were that horse I'd break away
And run to the hills across the brook
And never take a backward look
At the man who put me in such a place.

II

Sweet single rose, gnarled pear tree,
Stair with a broken tread,
Are all that is left of the house and yard.
Those who lived with them are dead
Or, maybe, gone beyond the mountain.
On every road, we pass
Old houses lost in the grass.
Walk slowly now and with care.
Watch for the well and the cellar door,
For boards, rotting there.
Nothing that's near can pull you out.
Nobody will ever hear your shout.

BIRDS IN THE CHIMNEY

That noise in the chimney must be wings of birds
Fluttering and turning; rising now and falling
Like a sudden gust of wind, bred in the chimney,
While the air stands still outside. There is no calling,
No twittering even. Swifts are strange birds,
Coming and going, on visits brief and slight,
With sounds almost forgotten till they come again,
Turning and fluttering in their narrow flight.

WOVEN WATER

Close to the bridge a bent limb has broken
The flowing pattern of the stream, whose lines
Are curved into a fabric of links shaken
Like a net on the water, bright as the smooth designs
Woven in metals. The small fish swim beneath,
Fearing no shape or shimmer water takes.
The links are firm, the fabric feels no breath
Of wind as the swift current bends and breaks.

Now

Now the hay is cut, we can walk wherever we please
Across the fields and down to the fringe of trees
Marking a path of water, where the roots drink.
Now we can sit down on this hill and think
Of all the paths of water roads cross
Up here in the hills. Roads were first made, of course,
For men riding. They're not natural
Like brooks. To make a road there's trees to fell,
Earth to be moved and bridges spanning water;
But if I made a path that would scarcely stir
The flowers and weeds and crept around each bush,
Saying, as water does, "Hush! Hush!",
To trees and boulders, I might understand
A better way of living on the land.
It's plain that we must all have hay and such
For horse and cow in winter. I'd not ask much,
Just a wild place, like the brook, for walking the mind
Without a leash and never hearing behind
And beside it the cry, "Look out! Step back! Take care!"
Only the railroad crossings said, "Beware!",
When we were children. We ought to be glad that the hay
Has been cut and gathered up and stored away.

The group of poems "Only on the West Wind" was chosen for an award of $25.00,
among the short lyrics submitted for *The Bread Loaf Anthology*.

LEAP MINNOWS, LEAP

James Still

The minnows leap in drying pools.
In islands of water along the creekbed sands
They spring on drying tails, white bellies to the sun,
Gills spread, gills fevered and gasping.
The creek is sun and sand, and fish-throats rasping.

One pool has a peck of minnows. One living pool
Is knuckle deep with dying, a shrinking yard
Of glittering bellies. A thousand eyes look, look.
A thousand gills strain, strain the water-air.
There is plenty of water above the dam, locked and deep,
Plenty, plenty and held. It is not here.
It is not where the minnows spring with lidless fear.
They die as men die. Leap minnows, leap.

"Leap Minnows, Leap" first appeared in *The Saturday Review of Literature*.

OLD HORSE

Jessie V. Thayer

"Grow old along with me." That fits you well.
I in my prime, you in your first full strength,
That long-ago spring day I brought you home.
The man who wrote that didn't mean a horse.
Perhaps he might have, though, if he'd owned you.
For twenty years we've been contemporaries—
Now it is spring again and you are gone.

Each limber strap, each well-worn buckle hole,
Brings back some line of you familiar as
This hand, and flocking memories of your long
Allegiance; pride that only love could humble;
Your vices, too, that really were your virtues
Too sharply edged by the deep wheel-rut of time.

You championed all off-side prerogatives.
Concessions must be made nigh-side the neap;
That other had to be there,—you saw that—
To help hold up the neck yoke, but you held him
In low esteem. A nip for him—for me,
The understanding velvet of your nose.

You and I, always—*we* were the team!
To know each other's crotchets and respect them!
No innovations—proven ways were best—
Each year convinced you more and more of that.
We never did agree within two inches
On where a swath should end. For twenty summers,
Those two-inch tufts proclaimed the "better man."

Cranky and proud as ever you marched to your
Reward—testy because your stiff old knees
Would not obey the quick-step of your spirit.
A good end—swift death between the eyes
And a deep grave. No pensioned ease for you—
You hated idleness. You would have seen
Through it, and seeing, it would have galled your pride.

Well—I'll have to change this harness some,
In places. The land lies waiting for the plow.

GENESIS

Louis Untermeyer

The lesser things were done. He had employed
Light to relieve the overwhelming void.

Swishing his hands in elemental mist,
He gave the galaxy a casual twist,

Quartered the seasons, balanced night and day,
Started each sun on its determined way,

Tipped a half-moon above the seven seas,
His mind confused with elephants and fleas,

Pointed the earth with its peculiar features:
Mountains, moles, men, and all the nobler creatures.

But this was child's play. Soon he must begin.
He pushed a grass-blade up, and rubbed his chin.

Now was the moment for Creation. Now,
Wrinkling his bland and universal brow,

Now, desperate and grimly undeterred,
The Lord began to build the first small word.

JOSEPH BATTELL REPLIES TO A SOUTHERN CORRESPONDENT

Viola C. White

To Henry Clayton Willoughby, Esquire,
Georgia, at Possum Poke, in Possum Lane,—
For so, dear Sir, I send the answer back
To your epistle that with generous scope
Addressed me at "Vermont" alone, and came
Direct as homing pigeon. Sir, be sure
That I remember you, that I recall
Our one and memorable meeting, where
Our long climb brought us to the mountain top
With nothing to complain of in the site
Or in the company, except the storm
That made our words together less than monks'
Bound with a vow to silence; for the storm
Outshouted us, while we climbed ridge by ridge,
Watchful and competent and voiceless; there
The rocks set wide apart gave evidence
Of what men's steps could be, even as the storm
Of what their talk could not. And then you passed
With friendly gesture down the western slope
And I the eastern, not to meet till now.
"Joseph Battell, Vermont" from you renews,
With memory, desire for the speech
Denied by Mother Nature when we met.

Indeed your query reads as large and fine
As your address. You want to know the man
You stood with on the stormy mountain height;
And I am leaving, skewered on their spike,
A flock of little notes on stocks and bonds,
Subscriptions and reports, to answer you.

Joseph Battell, Vermont,—what he may be,—
His faith, his family, his work, his plans.
My faith, not orthodox, though God and Man
Form its two pillars. For my family,
I am not married, Sir; that time we stood
Where the wind tried to blow us off the top
No woman in the valley looked with fear
Through darkening glass, trying to guess my fate.
Yet think me not a crusty bachelor,
For Woman as life principle I trace
In all that lives. When as a boy I set
My nimble feet upon the old world trails
I never watched the ground too close to miss
The girl who like a deer leaped on the rocks
Ahead; and in the deep blue Rhone I saw
Swiss maidens, on its banks reflected there,
And thought the lovely water lovelier still.
In brief, I hold the oak not less an oak
But more an oak, for the dryad at its heart.

Beauty of woman and of Nature,—tree
And woman, these together, not apart,
Together make the meaning of the world.
In my laborious volume I have tried
To pack most of my own philosophy
To try to make this clear. The Whispering Pine
And Ellen are the symbols of my thought.
(A copy of the book shall go to you.)
Wordsworth upon this subject, or Rousseau,
Would make the pine give lessons to the girl.
I hold that Ellen, as a mortal child,
The heir of Man who is the heir of God,
Takes higher place within creation's scale.
She tells the secrets of the universe

In talk with the old pine. Of life and death
And life beyond, of matter and of mind,
They talk. She tells him motion is a part
Of matter, and she speculates on size
As wholly relative, both in itself
And to ourselves; no absolute exists
Of fast or yet of slow, all things that move
Being relative to the perceiver's view.
I doubt not some philosopher to come
Will make such thoughts a system,—since the styles
Of thought, like fashion, come around again,—
And say them better than sweet Ellen did.
Faith—family—checked off, and work. For plans—
I am no modern, Sir; the Morgan herd
Still feeds upon my pasture. Horses draw
My carriages. They shall not find themselves
Turned to museum pieces, while I steer
A horseless carriage, reeking gasoline
Instead of fragrant breath, with ominous horn
Like cries from someone it has flattened out,
And grim disaster running in its train.
The newspaper I own, the *Register*,
Is kept informed of all the accident,
Death and destruction brought by motor cars.
I spread the facts, allowing a full page,
And solidly they fill it every week.
I plan a countryside unmechanized,
Secure for woodlands and for horses still.
My dream is not of vacant wilderness,
But Nature's unspoiled beauty, gazed upon
By eyes that comprehend it. I have dreamed,
When like some early god I walked the slope
Of mountains I have bought but never earned,
Companion of the sunset, I would leave

159

To my staunch little college in the hills
This virgin forest, for a heritage.
What could I give them better than the site
Of snow in six-month sleep, of evergreen
Rising unhewn from the spongy forest floor?
And for my town, which eight times voted me
Its representative, I mean to leave
The hill that rises northeast of the town,
Standing alone, not risen like the rest
From range upheaval, but from glacial drift,
The kame called Chipman Hill; upon it grow
Rare flowers like ram's horn orchid, and there sings
The hermit thrush in rainy green twilight.
The rabbit and the skunk go free, the deer
Sets in steep ice his narrow heart-shaped track.
And so it shall remain. I cannot ward
From my own body when the hour strikes
Death and decay, but for the hills I can,—
For the body of the hills,—prolong their life,
Give seasons, moons of years, and years unchanged,—
What seems an immortality compared
To a man's stay on earth.
I know well what my fellow townsmen want.
If they could have a bare scalped dome on top
Of Chipman where the trees would grow as few
As hairs upon an Indian's head, and stand
In geometric pattern, clipped with shears,
With a paved square laid out, and white stone urns
Bulging like those that held the Forty Thieves
They'd think they had a pretty park up there,
And point with pride to my beneficence.
They will not get it. I'll bequeath the hill,
With the inextricable interdict
That keeps the forest growing. Still the snake

Shall raise his black head from the fallen leaves
Of autumn, and the pine trees drop in spring
Their yellow pollen on the deepening mold.

I must not let the "substance of things hoped"
Which are not yet become reality
Deter me longer from the present wish
That you, dear Sir, if ever you draw near
To Joe Battell, Vermont, will surely come
Again to join me on a mountain top.
And I will harness up my Morgan span
And gladly sweeping down the Gorge, will bring
My guest with me to Bread Loaf. We have stood
On high ground once together, Sir, and may
Again, to keep the memory ever green.

THE SHINING PREY

Anthony Wrynn

Pheasant, prince in your intricate home of twig and bough,
Despiser of the dull ground, whose airy estates
Are soundless, wide, in light, move one concealing leaf
And the gun will speak from the umbrage.

Your feathers, tapering tier into dappled tier
From your reared head to the final scimitar of your tail,
Shine softly in the green sun
As you sit motionless in the unreality of fear.

Dominate the finger on the unseen lock.
Brood down the booted prowler who kneels before you
Only to see you beat your wings in blood and fall
Throbbing upon the ground, your crest in stones.

Wait, pheasant, the sharp impatience of his greed.
Wait, before you ease your golden claws, the wrathful step,
The vanishing curse hurled to appease
The loss of your hidden splendour of flesh and feather.

"The Shining Prey" first appeared in *Poetry*.

AN ABANDONED SETTLEMENT

Anthony Wrynn

This land sweeps cold and narrow into the rainy sea.
Wind-smoothed dunes rise grey in the drifting light
And the breakers' foam slides angrily up the sand.
Only in jagged streaks of grass spring visits here.

Gulls prowl the mist, crying, hunting the tides.
The sea in predatory stream explores the dunes,
From shell to root, and soon will be the land.
Half sunk and blind the houses are home for mildew,

Centipede and wind. They lie like driven hulks.
Ignorant laughter, ignorant lust and death,
Once lived safe and warm within those walls.
A gaunt forgotten lighthouse rises here,

Leaning toward the shoals it has betrayed.
Suddenly, with slow gigantic lurch, it will crash down,
Its black stones staggering into the waves.
Why does my heart cry out, This is my own place!

"An Abandoned Settlement" first appeared in *Poetry*.

SAINT JOHN IN THE WILDERNESS

Anthony Wrynn

Naked as anger you came among the rocks and briars,
Like another beast, eating locusts and honey
From storm-bleached hives, putting on nettled skins
In the leaves, passionate, brooding, going to bed on the stones.

Wildly your words shook from your bearded mouth—"Dissolute man,
Gone at the heart, how you try to goad the sweetness of summer,
Wring rapture from a weed. Winter comes and your hand
Hurries among the constellations, seeking to twist the stars

In forged solution of your ruin as you fall in secret."
Who heard you there in the dismal rooms of the forest,
Wasting God's light in caves of dross and dust,
Who but the unconquerable rocks and trees?

Scholar you might have been to a later John who forced his torrents
Into a page he could not see, regiving paradise with careful word,
Who steered God's sun, filled with centuries of grain and flowers,
Upon the hungry furrows rotting in frost.

"St. John in the Wilderness," first appeared in *Poetry*.

BIOGRAPHIES

AMY BELLE ADAMS is a teacher of English at Mattanawcook Academy, Lincoln, Maine. Umcolcus Lake, the locale of her poem on an incident in the Aroostook War, is a short distance from her native town, Patten. She is a Phi Beta Kappa graduate of the University of Maine and attended the Bread Loaf School of English in 1938. Her poems have been published in *Driftwind*, *Sun-Up*, *Verse Craft*, *Expression*, the Hartford *Times*, Portland *Telegram*, Lewiston *Journal*, and several anthologies.

HERVEY ALLEN, author of *Anthony Adverse* and *Action at Aquila* was a lecturer and staff member at the Bread Loaf School of English and the Writers' Conference irregularly between 1926 and 1934. He was graduated from the University of Pittsburgh in 1915 and was a student at Harvard from 1920 to 1922. Among his books of poetry are: *Ballads of the Border* (1916); *Wampum and Old Gold* (1921); *The Bride of Huitzal* (1922); *Carolina Chansons* (1922); *The Blindman* (1923); *Earth Moods* (1925); *Sarah Simon* (1929); *New Legends* (1929). In addition to his more popularly known recent fiction he is author of the following prose works: *Towards the Flame* (1926); *Israfel* (1927); *Poe's Brother* (1927). A novel *Richfield Springs* is in process of completion.

FLORENCE BECKER's interests run from progressive education, the labor movement, and parent education to anthropology and psychoanalysis. She was graduated from Columbia University in 1925 and in 1938 attended the Bread Loaf Writers' Conference where she was awarded first prize in poetry competition. She now lives in New York City. Her poetry has appeared in the New York *World* (Conning Tower), *Contempo*, *Modern Monthly*, *New Republic*, *Plebs* (London), *Saturday Review of Literature*, *Social Frontier*, *University Review* (Kansas City), *Upward*, and *Voices*; also in the anthologies *May Days* (1925), *American Caravan* (1927); *Moult's Best Poems of 1937*, and the 1938 *New England Anthology*. Her first book *Farewell to Walden*, a sequence of forty-nine sonnets, will be published in the summer of 1939, by the Exiles' Press.

MARY ELIZABETH BURTIS was graduated from Middlebury in 1929. Since graduation she has been in turn a typist in an insurance company, a graduate student in Union Theological Seminary, a member of the Bread Loaf Writers' Conference (1931), a graduate student in English at Radcliffe, a traveller in the United States, and a free lance. At present Miss Burtis is living in Orange, N. J., and completing work for a Master of Arts degree in English at Columbia.

MILDRED FERGUSON COUSENS was born in Portland, Connecticut, in 1904. She was graduated from Radcliffe College in 1928 with honors in English and for one year taught in the Dalton High School, Dalton, Mass. Since her marriage in 1929 to Theodore Wells Cousens, Associate Professor of Government and Law at Lafayette College, she has lived in Easton, Pennsylvania, spending her summers in Maine. *The World Tomorrow*, *American Mercury*, *The American Scholar*, and *The Saturday Review of Literature* are among the magazines which have published her poetry. She attended the Bread Loaf Writers' Conference in 1937.

KILE CROOK (EDWARD L. CROOK) lives in Durham, Connecticut, where he is employed by the Connecticut Department of Labor. He published light verse in the old *Life* (under Sherwood's editorship), *College Humor* and other magazines. Poems have appeared in *Smoke, Poetry*, the New York *Times*, the New York *Sun*, *North American Review*, *American Scholar*, *Saturday Review of Literature*, *Scribner's*, *Sewanee Review*, and other periodicals. He was a Fellow at the Bread Loaf Writers' Conference in 1936.

CHRISTINE TURNER CURTIS, North Abington, Mass., a graduate of Wellesley College, took special English courses at Boston University under Dallas Lore Sharp, and attended the Bread Loaf Writers' Conference in 1931. She has been connected with several publishing houses, both in publicity and editorial work, notably Macmillan Co., The Outlook Co., F. A. Stokes Co., and Ginn & Co. She has recently been employed in the writing and translating of lyrics for the new WORLD OF MUSIC SERIES published by Ginn & Co. Miss Curtis spent a year and a half in Santa Barbara, California, as publicity director of the Community Arts Association, and her short novel *Amarilis* has a California setting. Another volume, called *Nip and Tuck* is a picture book for children, with poems translated from the German. Miss Curtis has had articles in *The Saturday Review of Literature, Commonweal, Christian Science Monitor*, and poems in the *Canadian Forum, Saturday Review of Literature, Nation*, University of California *Chronicle*, Wellesley *Alumnae Quarterly, House Beautiful*, Boston *Transcript*, etc.

DONALD DAVIDSON, a native Tennessean, is a professor of English at Vanderbilt University. He has been a member of the Bread Loaf staff since 1931. His books include: *Outland Piper* (1924); *The Tall Men* (1937); *The Attack on Leviathan: Regionalism and Nationalism in the United States* (1938); *Lee in the Mountains* (1938); and *British Poetry of the 1890's* (1937) which he edited. His essays have appeared in anthologies such as: *I'll Take My Stand* (1930); *Culture in the South* (1934); *Who Owns America* (1936).

WILFRED DAVISON was the most vital force in the establishment of the Bread Loaf School of English, serving as Dean of the School from 1921–29. He is the author of the general plan on which the School and Conference still operate. Following his graduation from Middlebury in 1913 he served as Instructor and Assistant Professor of German until 1918 when he became a member of the English department. He was professor of American Literature from 1921 to the time of his death in 1929. One of Middlebury's greatest teachers, his energy and time were devoted more to the teaching of courses in American poetry and expression than to his own composition of verse.

ROBERT ALLISON EVANS's family has been connected with the Anthracite industry in Pennsylvania for a century. He holds a certificate as a miner and as a mine foreman; was chief mining engineer of one of the largest coal producers, and a mine executive for many years. He is now engaged as consulting mining engineer in New York City and Scranton, Pa.; has written technical articles for *Coal Age* and published many reports on the coal industry. His books include one novel *Royalties Due*, and a book of verse *Below the Grass Roots*. Poems have been published in *The New Masses*, and verse, biography, editorial material and book reviews in *The New Republic*. He was awarded first prize for fiction at the Bread Loaf Writers' Conference, 1937.

168

KIMBALL FLACCUS was graduated from Dartmouth College in 1933 and the following year received his M.A. from Columbia University. At present he teaches Public Speaking at the College of the City of New York, and is a candidate for the Ph.D. degree at New York University. The winter of 1934–35 he spent in Ireland on a fellowship from Dartmouth, and he is considered an authority on Irish history and literature. Scribner's published his first book of poems, *Avalanche of April*, in 1934. He attended the Bread Loaf Writers' Conference in 1931. He is at present on the Executive Board of The Poetry Society of America and contributes poems to the better periodicals, and occasional feature articles and book reviews to the New York *Sun*.

ROBERT FRANCIS is a graduate of Harvard, class of 1923, and has the degree of Ed.M. from the Harvard Graduate School of Education. For two years he taught in secondary schools, but now divides his time between music teaching and writing at Amherst, Massachusetts. In 1936 he was a fellow at the Bread Loaf Writers' Conference. Most of his published verse is included in two volumes published by Macmillan: *Stand With Me Here* (1936) and *Valhalla and Other Poems* (1938).

FRANCES FROST is the author of five books of poetry: *Hemlock Wall* (1929); *Blue Harvest* (1931); *These Acres* (1932); *Pool in the Meadow* (1933); *Woman of This Earth* (1934); and two novels: *Innocent Summer* (1936) and *Yoke of Stars* (1939). Miss Frost is a frequent contributor of verse and fiction to the *New Yorker*, *American Mercury*, the *Saturday Evening Post* and other magazines. She was born in St. Albans, Vt., in 1905, attended Middlebury College 1923–1926, and in 1931 received a Ph.B. from the University of Vermont, where she was an Instructor in Creative Poetry for two years. She now lives in New York City.

ROBERT M. GAY was a member of the Bread Loaf School of English staff from 1925 to 1936, Dean from 1930 to 1934 and Director 1935–1936. He was also Director of the Writers' Conference 1929–1931. Since 1918 he has been professor of English at Simmons College, Dean of the Graduate Division 1922–1935, Director of the School of English since 1933, and Chairman of the Division of Language, Literature and Arts since 1935. Among his books are: *Writing Through Reading* (1920); *Emerson—A Study of the Poet as Seer* (1928); *Reading and Writing* (1935); he is the compiler of *College Book of Verse* (1927); and *College Book of Prose* (1929). The *Atlantic Monthly* frequently publishes his essays.

EDNA GOEDEN teaches English at Washington High School, Milwaukee, Wisconsin. She has held jobs as sales clerk, canvasser, recreation worker, and waitress. She is a graduate, A.B., M.A., from Marquette University, Milwaukee. The summers of 1937 and 1938 were spent at the Bread Loaf School of English and the Writers' Conference. She has written a number of short stories, not yet published, and is at present working on a novel. Her poetry has appeared in the New York *Times*, *American Prefaces*, the *English Journal*, and *Spirit*.

JORGE GUILLEN is the outstanding contemporary poet of Spain. He was a member of the Middlebury College faculty in 1938 and is Visiting Professor of the Middlebury Spanish School for 1939. Among the great Universities of Europe where he has lectured or served as Professor are: Madrid, Murcia, Granada, Santander, Seville, Oxford, Cambridge, Paris, Bucarest, Iasi and Cluj (Roumania). He has been a contributor to the principal Spanish literary reviews since 1920 and has published three volumes of poetry in Spain. His work has been translated into English, German, French, and Italian.

ROBERT HILLYER was a member of the Bread Loaf Writers' Conference staff in 1932, 1933, and 1936. He was graduated from Harvard in 1917 and since 1919 has been a member of the English Department of Harvard except for the two years 1926–1928 when he was an Assistant Professor of English at Trinity College. Among his books of poems are: *Sonnets and Other Lyrics* (1917); *Alchemy—A Symphonic Poem* (1920); *The Hills Give Promise* (1923); *The Coming Forth by Day* (1923); *The Halt in the Garden* (1925); *The Happy Episode* (1927); *The Seventh Hill* (1928); *The Gates of the Compass* (1930); *Collected Verse* (1933). He is a frequent contributor of verse and essays to magazines and the author of one novel *Riverhead*. In 1934 he was awarded the Pulitzer prize in poetry.

DORIS MCLAURY HUGHSON was graduated in 1927 from Wells College where she studied under Robert P. Tristram Coffin. After two years of teaching high school English she married and settled in Oneonta, N. Y., thirteen miles from her native village of Portlandville on the Susquehanna River. In 1931 she attended the Bread Loaf Writers' Conference and has since written a narrative poem dealing with rural life fifty years ago. Her verse has appeared in F.P.A.'s column, Edward Hope's column, Clarence Peaslee's *Attic Salt*, *The Holstein-Friesian World*, and in *The Second Book of Wells Verse*.

CHRISTIE FRANCES JEFFRIES, a member of the English faculty of the New Jersey State Teachers College in Paterson, N. J., is a native Missourian. She is a graduate of the University of Missouri with the degree of Master of Arts and has done advanced work in English at Harvard. In 1935, she attended the Writers' Conference at Boulder, Colorado, and in 1937 was a contributing member at the Bread Loaf Writers' Conference. Poems by Miss Jeffries have appeared in *Voices, Spirit, Opinion*, the New York *Times*, the New York *Sun, Cleveland Club Woman, Literary Digest*, the Dallas *News*, the Augusta *Chronicle*, the Pasadena *Star-News, The Challenge, Kaleidograph, Poetry World, Expression, Versecraft, Literary America*, and in various other periodicals and anthologies.

BURGES JOHNSON began his literary career, after graduation from Amherst in 1899, with the New York *Evening Post*, and the *Commercial Advertiser* under Lincoln Steffens. From newspaper work he found his way into editing and publishing, serving as literary adviser to such publishing houses as G. P. Putnam's Sons and E. P. Dutton & Co., and on the editorial staffs of various magazines, including several years with Harpers. He gradually dropped his editorial connections in New York during eleven years of teaching at Vassar, later went to Syracuse University, and now heads the English Department at Union College. He has been a visiting lecturer at many colleges and universities, with summer teaching in California, Colorado, Arizona, and at the Bread Loaf School of English. For many years he has been a contributor to magazines chiefly essays and verse. Much of his work has been collected in book form. The best known are his *New Rhyming Dictionary*, *Professor at Bay* (essays), *Youngsters* (verses of childhood) and his volumes of verse about dogs.

HERBERT KRAUSE was born on a hill farm in Friberg, north of Fergus Falls, Minnesota, which he still calls home. He stayed in the ninth grade in the rural school four years because there were no grades higher and the law required pupils to attend school until they were sixteen. For the three years following he ran his father's farm, then teamed for a construction company. He was graduated *magna cum laude* from St. Olaf College in 1933. Having worked in advertising offices, newspaper rooms, banks, on farms, selling books, he entered the University of Iowa and took a master's degree in 1935, submitting a volume of verse for a thesis. He is now preparing for his Ph.D. at the same institution. He attended Bread Loaf School of English on a scholarship in 1935. Bobbs-Merrill Company published his novel *Wind Without Rain*, which won the $1000 Friends of American Writers Award for 1939, annually given by a Chicago literary group for the best mid-western novel of the year. He has written a play *Bondsmen to the Hills*, and has contributed verse to such magazines as *American Prefaces* and such anthologies as Colman's *Contemporary Poets*, *Muse*, *Minnesota Poets*, and *Contemporary American Poets*. He is now head of the English Department, Augustana College, Sioux Falls, South Dakota.

MARION LEEPER is an associate professor of English in Northern Montana College. She has a Bachelor's degree from the University of Washington and a Master's degree from Mills College. She has done graduate work in the University of Colorado, the University of Washington, the University of California, Mills College, Columbia University, and Oxford. Miss Leeper attended the Writers' Conference at Bread Loaf in 1935. Her poems have been published in the *University of Washington Book of Poems*, the *Frontier and Midland*, *Harpers*, and the *Northwest Anthology of Verse*.

LOUISE MCNEILL was born in Marlinton, W. Va. She attended West Virginia University, Concort College, Ohio State University, and Miami University where she received an M.A. in 1938. As recipient of the *Atlantic Monthly* Fellowship, she spent the summer of 1938 at the Bread Loaf School of English. She is now Associate Editor of *American Prefaces* and is working on her doctorate at the University of Iowa. Her poems have been published in *American Mercury*, *Saturday Evening Post*, *Forum*, *Poetry*. *Mountain White*, a book of verse, was published by Kaleidoscope Press, Dallas, Texas, in 1931. She has worked on a newspaper and taught school in West Virginia.

CHARLES MALAM, a native of St. Johnsbury, Vt., graduated from Middlebury College in 1928, studied at Oxford the following year on a Middlebury fellowship and in 1929 received a Rhodes Scholarship appointment. His first book of poems *Spring Plowing* was published while he was an undergraduate and was followed by *Upper Pasture* in 1930. His novels are *City Keep* (1931), and *Slow Smoke* (1931). He attended the Bread Loaf School of English from 1927 to 1930 and the Writers' Conference in 1927 and 1928. He is now employed in Brooklyn, N. Y.

JEANNETTE CONSTANCE MARTIN is a student at Middlebury College where she is considered one of the outstanding undergraduate authors. She has attended both the

171

Bread Loaf School of English and the Writers' Conference. In close succession she has lived in Ohio, Florida, New York, and Vermont. Her poems have appeared in several magazines and newspapers as well as in Middlebury College publications.

MARGUERITE ENID MORGAN was born in Plymouth, Pa., of Welsh parentage. Her father was a minister and the family moved about a great deal during her youth, settling at last in a town in New England. She attended Northfield Seminary and Simmons College where she majored in English. She attended the Bread Loaf School of English and the Writers' Conference in the summer of 1938, following her graduation. In September, 1938, she started work as assistant to the editor of Harweal, Inc., publishers of limited editions, and is now employed as advertising manager of the American Art Alloys, Inc., New York City. For three consecutive years Miss Morgan has won the literary contest sponsored by the New England Federation of Women's Clubs. She has had poetry published in *Versecraft*, *Poet Lore*, *Modern Poetry*, *The Bard*, and *Saturday Review of Literature*.

THEODORE MORRISON has been Director of the Bread Loaf Writers' Conference since 1932. Shortly after his graduation from Harvard in 1923 he was appointed an associate editor of *The Atlantic Monthly* and remained on the staff of the magazine until 1931. He is now an Assistant Professor of English at Harvard. Most of his poetry has been published in the two volumes: *The Serpent in the Cloud*, and *Notes of Death and Life*.

FRED LEWIS PATTEE was a member of the Bread Loaf English School staff from 1924 through 1936. He is one of the leading scholars of American literature. Among his works are *The Wine of May and Other Lyrics* (1893); *Pasquaney* (1894); *A History of American Literature* (1896); *Foundations of English Literature* (1900); *Mary Garvin* (1902); *The House of the Black Ring* (1905); *Elements of Religious Pedagogy* (1909); *The Breaking Point* (1911); *Compelled Men* (1913); *History of American Literature Since 1870* (1915); *Sidelights on American Literature* (1922); *Development of the American Short Story* (1923); *Tradition and Jazz* (1924); *The New American Literature* (1930). He has also edited anthologies and texts on Shakespeare, Freneau, American literature and Mark Twain. He was a professor of American Literature at Pennsylvania State College 1894–1928 and has since been at Rollins College, Florida. He was at the Blowing Rock Summer School of English, N. C., 1937, 1938.

SAMUEL B. PETTENGILL, former congressman from Indiana, was graduated from Middlebury in 1908. Three years later he received his law degree from Yale and has since been practicing law in South Bend, Indiana. He represented his state in Washington from 1931–1939. He is author of two books: *Hot Oil* and *Jefferson, the Forgotten Man*.

HAZEL BISHOP POOLE is a high school teacher of English in Newark, N. J. She received her A.B. from Vassar, and her A.M. from Bread Loaf, where she attended the School of English from 1924–1927, and 1935–1937, and the Writers' Conference from 1929–1931. She has also studied at Oxford and at Stanford University, and has taught summer session classes at Rutgers University and at the Blowing Rock School of English.

MADELINE REEDER (THURSTON) was born in Ogden, Utah, and has since lived in almost all of the forty-eight states of the Union. Her poetry has been praised by Harriet

Monroe, Ridgely Torrence and others. She has written for newspapers, edited library bulletins, painted backdrops for ballets, and written novels, the first of which is now ready for print. For the past four years she has been married to Jarvis A. Thurston who teaches mathematics and is book editor of the Ogden *Standard-Examiner*. Miss Reeder attended the Writers' Conference in 1933.

PEDRO SALINAS is a leading contemporary scholar and poet of Spain. For the past three years he has been lecturing in American universities, notably Johns Hopkins, and Middlebury, where he was for two summers Visiting Professor in the Spanish School and recipient of an honorary doctorate in literature in 1937. Since 1936 he has been Professor at Wellesley College. He was Director of the course for foreign students in the Centro de Estudios Históricos of Madrid from 1928–31, and Director of the Contemporary Literature division of the same institution from 1932–1936. Among the many European universities where he has lectured are: Paris, Seville, Cambridge, Madrid, Santander, Oxford, Brussells, Hamburg, Berlin, Bonn, and Cologne. Since 1913 he has been a frequent contributor to the principal Spanish literary reviews and has published five volumes of poetry.

LEOTA ESTELLA SCHOFF was born in Colebrook, N. H. She attended Maine Wesleyan Seminary and Colby College from which she was graduated in 1925. Subsequent to graduation she taught three years in the South, and since that time has been head of the English Department in the Alonzo K. Learned High School, Holden, Mass. She attended the Bread Loaf School of English in 1937 and 1938. Her verse has appeared in *The Baptist*, *Zion's Herald*, and *Opportunity* and she is the author of a one-act play "The Kid Brother."

DALLAS LORE SHARP (1870–1929), author, naturalist, and Boston University professor for thirty years, taught at the Bread Loaf School of English from 1927 to 1929. Acclaimed at the turn of the century as a "new naturalist-poet," he left his greatest imprint as a nature writer, educator, and lecturer. In all he published twenty books. Among his later works are: *Sanctuary! Sanctuary!*, *The Better Country*, and *Boy's Life of John Burroughs*, and the posthumous volumes, *Romances from the Old Testament*, and *Christ and His Time*.

ISRAEL SMITH, Jersey Shore, Pa., attended Middlebury College 1931–1933. He has lived in Pennsylvania, Washington, D. C., Massachusetts, and Vermont, and has been at various times a private research assistant in the Library of Congress, a free-lance journalist, and for two years assistant to the director of the Middlebury Community House. At present he is working on the manuscript of a novel with a Vermont background. His poetry has appeared in *Poetry*, *The American Poetry Journal*, the New York *Times*, *Smoke*, *The English Journal*, and various other magazines.

FLORIDA WATTS SMYTH began a literary career with a private publication of lyric verse and poems of travel written between the ages of twelve and twenty. After marriage at twenty she wrote nothing for thirty years, most of that time being spent in travel abroad, in the western states, in Hawaii and the Orient. Returning to a quiet country home after this interval, she began to write again and has had contributions in *Poetry*, *Contemporary Verse*, *The Lyric*, *Literary Digest*, New York *Times*, *London Poetry Review*, *The*

173

Commonweal, and other general publications. This verse includes metaphysical lyrics and longer pieces on pioneer themes and the great central rivers. She received a Poetry Society of America Prize in 1936 and attended the Bread Loaf Writers' Conference from 1935 through 1938, receiving the prize for Poetry there in 1936 and 1937. She has also attended the Bread Loaf School of English since 1936 and has been a student at both Washington and Columbia Universities.

JAMES STILL was born in the Buckalew Mountains of Alabama. He attended Vanderbilt University and the University of Illinois. For the past six years he has been librarian of the Hindman Settlement School, a pioneer educational institution at the forks of Troublesome Creek in the Kentucky Mountains. *Hounds on the Mountain*, a volume of poems, was published in 1937 (Viking). His poems and short stories have appeared in *The Yale Review*, *The Nation*, *The Atlantic Monthly*, *Story*, *The New Republic*, *The Virginia Quarterly Review*, *The Saturday Review of Literature*, *Poetry*, *The Sewanee Review*, *Esquire*, *The Saturday Evening Post*, F.P.A.'s "Conning Tower," etc. He was represented in the O. Henry Memorial Prize volumes for 1937 and 1938, and received a Bread Loaf Writers' Conference fellowship in 1937.

JESSIE V. THAYER of Amherst, Mass., is a farmwife and mother. She was graduated from Smith College in 1906 and attended the Bread Loaf Writers' Conference in 1934. Writing is her avocation only. A few of her stories, essays, and poems have appeared in Massachusetts newspapers and in the Smith *Quarterly*.

LOUIS UNTERMEYER, America's most widely known poet-anthologist, lectured at Bread Loaf in 1922 and 1925 and has since been a frequent visitor there. Among his most enduring volumes are *Challenge* (1914); *Roast Leviathan* (1923); *Burning Bush* (1928); and *Selected Poems and Parodies* (1935). His anthologies include: *This Singing World* (1923); *Yesterday and Today* (1927); several editions of *Modern American Poetry* and *Modern British Poetry*; *American Poetry from the Beginning to Whitman* (1931); *The Book of Living Verse* (1932); *Rainbow in The Sky* (1935); and *Doorways to Poetry* (1938). His Henry Ward Beecher lectures at Amherst were published under the title *Play in Poetry* (1938). His home is now at Elizabethtown, N. Y., in the Adirondack Mountains.

VIOLA C. WHITE is Curator of the Abernethy Collection of American Literature at Middlebury College. She received her B.A. degree from Wellesley, M.A. from Columbia University, and Ph.D. from the University of North Carolina. *The Nation*, *Survey*, *Voices* are among the magazines in which her poetry has appeared and the *Atlantic Monthly* has published both essays and poems by her. She is the author of three volumes of poetry: *Horizons*, *The Hour of Judgment*, and *Blue Forest*. *Horizons* was the first volume by a woman to appear in the Yale Series of Younger Poets.

ANTHONY WRYNN, Brooklyn, N. Y., has been a pianist, commercial artist, and actor, has worked in forestry camps, and in the merchant marine. He received a fellowship to the Bread Loaf Writers' Conference in 1936. His poetry has appeared in *The Dial*, *Poetry*, *The Little Review*, *The Measure*, *Rhythmus*, and in various anthologies and newspapers; his short stories in *The Dial*. A short story which won the Bread Loaf Writers' Conference award in 1936 and several poems were published in book form under the title *Someone Who Will Not Believe It*, by Ritten House, donor of the award. At present he is working on the manuscript of a volume of poems and on a novel.

174